EVERYMAN,
I WILL GO WITH THEE
AND BE THY GUIDE,
IN THY MOST NEED
TO GO BY THY SIDE

EVERYMAN'S LIBRARY
POCKET POETS

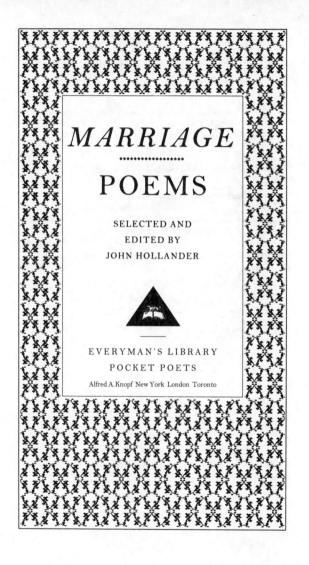

MARRIAGE

···················

POEMS

SELECTED AND
EDITED BY
JOHN HOLLANDER

EVERYMAN'S LIBRARY
POCKET POETS

Alfred A. Knopf   New York   London   Toronto

THIS IS A BORZOI BOOK
PUBLISHED BY ALFRED A. KNOPF

This selection by John Hollander first published in
Everyman's Library, 1997
Copyright © 1997 by Everyman's Library

Eighth printing (US)

A list of acknowledgments to copyright owners appears at the back of
this volume.

US website: www.randomhouse.com/everymans

ISBN 0-679-45515-9 (US)
1-85715-732-X (UK)

A CIP catalogue record for this book is available from the British Library

Typography by Peter B. Willberg

Typeset in the UK by AccComputing, North Barrow, Somerset

Printed and bound in Germany by GGP Media GmbH, Pössneck

CONTENTS

Foreword 13

COURTSHIP AND ENGAGEMENT

ANONYMOUS
    I Shall Be Married on Monday Morning . .   17

THEOCRITUS The Suitor 19

ANONYMOUS (BOJPURI) Her Father's House 24

EDMUND SPENSER To Her Doubts 25

GEORGE MEREDITH Love in the Valley 26

EDWARD LEAR The Owl and the Pussy-Cat 30

ROBERT BROWNING My Last Duchess 32

EDNA ST. VINCENT MILLAY The Betrothal 35

WEDDINGS

ALFRED, LORD TENNYSON Marriage Morning . . 39

D. H. LAWRENCE Wedding Morn 40

THOMAS HARDY The Wedding Morning 42

From *The Song of Songs* The Bride Sings 43

RAINER MARIA RILKE The Bride 44

MUSAEUS The Marriage of Hero and Leander . . 45

ANONYMOUS Lord Thomas and Fair Eleanor . . 46

ANONYMOUS The Frog and the Mouse 49

JOHN DONNE Ceremonials 51

HENRY WADSWORTH LONGFELLOW
    Hiawatha's Wedding-Feast 54

5

WALT WHITMAN A Wedding Out West   56
DYLAN THOMAS On the Marriage of a Virgin . .   57
THOMAS HARDY At the Altar-Rail   58
LUCAN For a Remarriage   59
JAMES MERRILL Upon a Second Marriage   60
EDMUND WALLER On the Two Dwarfs That Were
    Married at Court   62
CHRISTOPHER SMART
    Epithalamium on a Late Happy Marriage . .   63
MATTHEW PRIOR To a Friend on His Nuptials . .   64
RICHARD WILBUR A Wedding Toast   65
EDMUND SPENSER Wedding Night   66
THOMAS HARDY A Beauty's Soliloquy during
    Her Honeymoon   69
RICHARD CRASHAW Harmony   71
THOMAS CAMPION
    Song ('Now hath *Flora* rob'd her bowers') . .   72
PHILIP LARKIN Wedding-Wind   74

DOMESTICITIES
ROSANNA WARREN Couple   77
EDWIN ARLINGTON ROBINSON Eros Turannos . .   79
ANONYMOUS (SANSKRIT) For Poorer   81
THOMAS HARDY At the Dinner-Table   82
                 A Question of Marriage   84
D. H. LAWRENCE The Painter's Wife   86
MOISHE LEIB HALPERN The Marriage   87

ROBERT HERRICK Upon One Lillie, Who Married
   with a Maid Call'd Rose 88
OVID The Story of Baucis and Philemon 89
RACHEL HADAS *From* Love 94
THOMAS HARDY She Revisits Alone the Church of
   Her Marriage 96
JONATHAN SWIFT The Progress of Marriage . . 98
THOMAS HARDY At Tea 105
ROBERT LOWELL
   'To Speak of Woe That Is in Marriage' 106
ANNE BRADSTREET
   Before the Birth of One of Her Children . . 107
JOHN MILTON Discourse 109
ROBERT FROST The Telephone 110
ROBERT HERRICK Upon Jolly and Jilly 111
GEORGE MEREDITH Modern Marriage 112
DANTE GABRIEL ROSSETTI Nuptial Sleep 113
EDNA ST. VINCENT MILLAY Witch-Wife 114
ROBERT FROST The Hill Wife 115
ROBERT BROWNING The Householder 119
ALFRED, LORD TENNYSON Tithonus 121

ANNIVERSARIES
ARTHUR HUGH CLOUGH Silver Wedding 127
SAMUEL BISHOP A Second Ring 130
WILLIAM BARNES Jeäne 132
DONALD JUSTICE On an Anniversary 133

DYLAN THOMAS On a Wedding Anniversary 134

YVOR WINTERS The Marriage 135

EDWIN MUIR The Commemoration 136

J. V. CUNNINGHAM To My Wife 138

ROBERT BURNS John Anderson My Jo 139

RICHARD CRASHAW
   An Epitaph upon Husband and Wife Who
   Died and Were Buried Together 140

ADULTERIES

JOHN DRYDEN A Foolish Marriage Vow 143

RUPERT BROOKE Menelaus and Helen 144

ANONYMOUS The Wraggle Taggle Gipsies . . . 146

ANONYMOUS
   (SPANISH) My Mother Made Me Marry . . 148

ANONYMOUS (INDIAN) The Flower-Girl 150

OVID The Art of Deceiving a Husband 151

THOMAS HARDY In the Restaurant 154

GEORGE MEREDITH Guests for Dinner 155

RUDYARD KIPLING Harp Song of the Dane Women 156

GEORGE MEREDITH The Triangle 158

JAMES DICKEY Adultery 160

ROBERT GRAVES Jus Primae Noctis 162

SEPARATIONS

JOHN DONNE
   A Valediction: Forbidding Mourning 165

EMPRESS IWA NO HIME

    Longing for the Emperor 167

WALLACE STEVENS The World as Meditation . . 168

CHIANG YEN Parting 170

KAKINOMOTO HITOMARO On Leaving His Wife . . 171

ANNE BRADSTREET A Letter to Her Husband,

    Absent upon Public Employment 173

EZRA POUND

    The River-Merchant's Wife: A Letter 175

ANONYMOUS (ANGLO-SAXON)

    The Wife's Lament 177

EDWIN MUIR Penelope in Doubt 180

JOHN HOLLANDER

    For Both of You, the Divorce Being Final . . 182

JULIAN (PREFECT OF EGYPT)

    For Anastasia's Grave 185

THOMAS HARDY In a London Flat 186

PROPERTIUS

    Cornelia from the Grave to Her Husband . . 188

HENRY KING On His Dead Wife 190

EDWIN ARLINGTON ROBINSON Reuben Bright 191

EDGAR LEE MASTERS Benjamin Pantier 192

                   Mrs. Benjamin Pantier 193

GEORGE WITHER A Widow's Hymn 194

RAINER MARIA RILKE The Song of the Widow . . 195

RUDYARD KIPLING The Widower 197

EDWARD COOTE PINKNEY The Widow's Song . . 198

JAMES WRIGHT Complaint 199
THOMAS HARDY Over the Coffin 200
JOHN MILTON Methought 201

SYMBOLIC MARRIAGES

WALLACE STEVENS Life is Motion 205
JAY MacPHERSON
    The Marriage of Earth and Heaven 206
EMILY DICKINSON
    The World Stands Solemner to Me 207
OMAR KHAYYÁM A New Wife 208
WILLIAM SHAKESPEARE Married Sounds 209
LI HO South Garden 210
RUDYARD KIPLING Jane's Marriage 211
DANTE GABRIEL ROSSETTI
    For a Marriage of St. Catherine by Memling 213
EMILY DICKINSON Title Divine 214

FOR AND AGAINST MARRIAGE

WILLIAM SHAKESPEARE
    'No Cause or Just Impediment' 217
PERCY BYSSHE SHELLEY The Dreariest Journey . . 218
ROBERT HERRICK
    To the Virgins, to Make Much of Time . . 219
ROBERT BROWNING The Real and True and Sure 220
WILLIAM SHAKESPEARE The Need of Posterity . . 221
SIR PHILIP SIDNEY A Word Against Wives 222

WILLIAM SHAKESPEARE Wasted Beauty 223
MARTIAL Warning to a Wife.. 224
WILLIAM CARLOS WILLIAMS The Marriage of Souls 226
GREGORY CORSO Marriage 227
ROBERT GRAVES Call It a Good Marriage 233
MONA VAN DUYN Toward a Definition of Marriage 234
LUCRETIUS The Way Things Are 240
PHILIP LARKIN Marriages 241

Acknowledgments 243

Index of Authors 249

11

FOREWORD

Marriage has been celebrated by poets since the beginning of history. In some societies, especially in classical times, poetry played a vital role in the processes of courtship and betrothal, and in the nuptial rites themselves. Throughout the world it has generated songs of praise and blessing in every age, like the extracts from the epithalamia by Donne and Spenser printed here.

But marriage can also be treated by poets in ways that are far from celebratory. Separations by distance and death, divorce and abandonment, unhappiness and frustration, have all had their bards. Indeed, poets – like novelists – often find what goes wrong in marriage more interesting than what stays right. In the seventeenth and eighteenth centuries this interest generated a whole genre of satiric verse, represented here by Swift's 'The Progress of Marriage'.

In the nineteenth century, poetry followed realistic fiction in its concern with married life after the wedding, for better or for worse. Hardy, Meredith and Lawrence could fill a volume between them on this topic. Twentieth-century writers have explored every aspect of the subject and contemporary poems, whether as exuberant as Gregory Corso's 'Marriage', or as wryly analytical as Mona Van Duyn's 'Toward a Definition of Marriage', revise earlier modes of wonder and meditation.

COURTSHIP AND ENGAGEMENT

'Lady Jingly! Lady Jingly!
'Sitting where the pumpkins blow,
'Will you come and be my wife?'
Said the Yonghy-Bonghy-Bò.
'I am tired of living singly, –
'On this coast so wild and shingly, –
'I'm a-weary of my life:
'If you'll come and be my wife,
'Quite serene would be my life!' –
Said the Yonghy-Bonghy-Bò,
Said the Yonghy-Bonghy-Bò.

EDWARD LEAR

I SHALL BE MARRIED ON MONDAY MORNING

As I was walking one morning in spring,
I heard a fair maiden most charmingly sing,
All under her cow, as she sat a-milking,
Saying, I shall be married, next Monday morning.

You fairest of all creatures, my eyes e'er beheld,
Oh! where do you live love, or where do you dwell,
I dwell at the top of yon bonny brown hill,
I shall be fifteen years old next Monday morning.

Fifteen years old love, is too young to marry,
The other five years love, I'd have you to tarry,
And perhaps in the meantime love you might be sorry,
So put back your wedding, next Monday morning.

You talk like a man without reason or skill,
Five years I've been waiting against my will,
Now, I am resolved my mind to fulfil,
I wish that tomorrow was Monday morning.

On Saturday night it is all my care,
To powder my locks and curl my hair,
And my two pretty maidens to wait on me there,
To dance at my wedding next Monday morning.

My husband will buy me a guinea gold ring,
And at night he'll give me a far better thing,
With two precious jewels he'll be me adorning,
When I am his bride, on Monday morning.

THE SUITOR

There was a passionate fellow who loved an unkind
    adolescent,
Decent enough in physique but his character wasn't
    in keeping,
For he detested his suitor and had no indulgence
    toward him,
Ignorant what a divinity Love is, how big are the shafts he
Wields in his hands and how sharp are the arrows he
    pierces the heart with.
He was immovable, whether by words or by other
    approaches,
Nor did he offer encouragement such as assuages the
    fires of
Love, not a twitch of the lip, not a gleam in his eyes
    or a rosy
Glow in his cheeks, not a word or a kiss to alleviate
    passion.
Just as a beast of the forest suspiciously glares at the
    huntsman,
So he regarded mankind altogether. His lips were
    farouche, and
Even his pupils possessed an inexorable, dreadful
    expression.
Often his face was completely transformed by extreme
    irritation,

And in his violent temper the colour deserted his
    features.
Yet even so he was beautiful, so that his anger excited
Rather his lover, who finally finding he could not
    endure the
Furious flame of the Love-goddess went and
    complained at the hateful
House of his love: after kissing the threshold he lifted
    his voice thus.
'Brutal, rebarbative boy, did a pitiless lioness nurse
    you,
Or are you fashioned of stone, so insensible are you to
    passion?
Now I have come with my ultimate gifts for you: here is
    the noose I'll
Use, for I do not desire to vex you, my lad, with the
    sight of
Me any longer. Instead I am going where you have
    condemned me –
There, it's alleged, is the sovereign cure for the
    sorrows of lovers,
Namely oblivion. Yet, if I lifted that drink to my lips
    and
Drank every drop of it, not even then should I quench
    my desire.
Finally, I am resigned to begin my adieux to your
    doorway,

Knowing the future. The rose is exquisite which time
    will extinguish;
Beautiful too in the Spring is the violet – quickly it ages!
White is the lily, and yet it is withered as soon as it
    flowers;
White as the snow is, moreover, it melts just as soon as
    it falls. The
Beauty of boyhood is beautiful also, and lives but a
    short while.
Sooner or later the moment will come when you feel as
    a lover
Does, when your heart is aflame, and the tears that you
    weep will be bitter.
Nevertheless, my dear boy, you can do me an ultimate
    kindness.
When you emerge from my house and discover my
    wretched cadaver
Dangling here in the doorway, do not I beseech you
    just pass me
By, but remain there and weep for me briefly, and when
    you have poured this
Tribute of tears, then unfasten the rope from me, wrap
    me in clothing
Stripped from your limbs and conceal me, and kiss me
    goodbye for the last time
Granting at least my dead body the grace of your lips.
    Do not fear me,

I am unable to harm you: by kissing me you will
  dismiss me.
Hollow a burial mound for me, one that will cover my
  love, and
At your departure address me three times, "You are
  resting in peace, friend."
And, if you like, you may add, "My attractive
  companion has perished."
Write this inscription I'm going to scrawl on the wall
  of your house, too.
"Love was the death of this personage. Traveller, do
  not continue,
But as you pause here remark, 'His companion was not
  sympathetic.'"'
When he had spoken he picked up a fatal stone and he
  placed it
Right in the midst of the entrance not far from the
  wall, and he fastened
Over the lintel a slender, dependable thread, and he
  put his
Neck in the noose, and he kicked the support from his
  foot and he hung there
Dead. But the boy when he opened the door and beheld
  the dead body
Hanged in his very own porch was completely
  untroubled in spirit,
Nor did he weep for the recent fatality. Rather, defiling

All of his juvenile garments he brushed by the body
    and went on
To the gymnasium with its athletic equipment, and
    calmly
Sought out his favourite part of the swimming pool,
    near where a statue
Stood of the god he had flouted. But just as he sprang
    from the marble
Pedestal into the water, the effigy toppled upon him,
Killing that bad adolescent. The water grew crimson.
    Above it
Echoed the voice of the dead boy: 'Lovers, rejoice! The
    disdainful
One is destroyed. Let disdainers be loving, for Love is a
    just god.'

HER FATHER'S HOUSE

Behind the father's house a cool wind
Stirs in the thick bamboo clump,
The father has put his bed in its shade
And is sound asleep.
Bending bending his daughter
Comes and upbraids him,
'With a girl not yet married in your house
How can you sleep so sound?'
'Sometimes I sleep, sometimes I wake,
Sometimes I worry over the dowry.
Daughter, until you are married,
I shall never sleep soundly.
Daughter, shake a mat
And welcome your father-in-law,
Worrying for your dowry
I cannot think what you should do.'
'Father, how shall I make the bed?
Where shall I put the mat?
Can you ever get me to a husband's house?
The dazzling moonlit night
Is shining on my forehead.'

ANONYMOUS, BOJPURI
TRANSLATED BY W. G. ARCHER

TO HER DOUBTS

The doubt which ye misdeem, fair love, is vain,
    That fondly fear to lose your liberty;
    When losing one, two liberties ye gain,
    And make him bond that bondage erst did fly.
Sweet be the bands, the which true love doth tie,
    Without constraint or dread of any ill:
    The gentle bird feels no captivity
    Within her cage, but sings and feeds her fill.
There pride dare not approach, nor discord spill
    The league twixt them that loyal love hath bound:
    But simple truth, and mutual good will,
    Seeks with sweet peace to salve each other's wound.
There faith doth fearless dwell in brazen tower,
And spotless pleasure builds her sacred bower.

LOVE IN THE VALLEY

Under yonder beech-tree standing on the green-sward,
  Couched with her arms behind her little head,
Her knees folded up, and her tresses on her bosom,
  Lies my young love sleeping in the shade.
Had I the heart to slide one arm beneath her,
  Press her dreaming lips as her waist I folded slow,
Waking on the instant she could not but embrace me –
  Ah! would she hold me, and never let me go?

Shy as the squirrel, and wayward as the swallow;
  Swift as the swallow when athwart the western flood
Circleting the surface he meets his mirrored winglets, –
  Is that dear one in her maiden bud.
Shy as the squirrel whose nest is in the pine-tops;
  Gentle – ah! that she were jealous as the dove!
Full of all the wildness of the woodland creatures,
  Happy in herself is the maiden that I love!

What can have taught her distrust of all I tell her?
  Can she truly doubt me when looking on my brows?
Nature never teaches distrust of tender love-tales,
  What can have taught her distrust of all my vows?
No, she does not doubt me! on a dewy eve-tide
  Whispering together beneath the listening moon,

I pray'd till her cheek flush'd, implored till she faltered –
   Fluttered to my bosom – ah! to fly away so soon!

When her mother tends her before the laughing
      mirror,
   Tying up her laces, looping up her hair,
Often she thinks – were this wild thing wedded,
   I should have more love, and much less care.
When her mother tends her before the bashful mirror,
   Loosening her laces, combing down her curls,
Often she thinks – were this wild thing wedded,
   I should lose but one for so many boys and girls.

Clambering roses peep into her chamber,
   Jasmine and woodbine breathe sweet, sweet,
White-necked swallows twittering of summer,
   Fill her with balm and nested peace from head to feet.
Ah! will the rose-bough see her lying lonely,
   When the petals fall and fierce bloom is on the leaves?
Will the Autumn garners see her still ungathered,
   When the fickle swallows forsake the weeping eaves?

Comes a sudden question – should a strange hand
      pluck her!
   Oh! what an anguish smites me at the thought.
Should some idle lordling bribe her mind with jewels! –
   Can such beauty ever thus be bought?

Sometimes the huntsmen prancing down the valley
    Eye the village lasses, full of sprightly mirth;
They see as I see, mine is the fairest!
    Would she were older and could read my worth!

Are there not sweet maidens if she still deny me?
    Show the bridal heavens but one bright star?
Wherefore thus then do I chase a shadow,
    Clattering one note like a brown eve-jar?
So I rhyme and reason till she darts before me –
    Thro' the milky meadows from flower to flower
        she flies,
Sunning her sweet palms to shade her dazzled eyelids
    From the golden love that looks too eager
        in her eyes.

When at dawn she wakens, and her fair face gazes
    Out on the weather thro' the window-panes,
Beauteous she looks! like a white water-lily
    Bursting out of bud on the rippled river plains.
When from bed she rises clothed from neck to ankle
    In her long nightgown, sweet as boughs of May,
Beauteous she looks! like a tall garden lily
    Pure from the night and perfect for the day!

Happy, happy time, when the grey star twinkles
    Over the fields all fresh with bloomy dew;

When the cold-cheeked dawn grows ruddy up
    the twilight,
  And the gold sun wakes, and weds her in the blue.
Then when my darling tempts the early breezes,
  She the only star that dies not with the dark!
Powerless to speak all the ardour of my passion
  I catch her little hand as we listen to the lark.

Shall the birds in vain then valentine their sweethearts?
  Season after season tell a fruitless tale;
Will not the virgin listen to their voices?
  Take the honeyed meaning, wear the bridal veil.
Fears she frosts of winter, fears she the bare branches?
  Waits she the garlands of spring for her dower?
Is she a nightingale that will not be nested
  Till the April woodland has built her bridal bower?

Then come merry April with all thy birds and beauties!
  With thy crescent brows and thy flowery, showery
    glee;
With thy budding leafage and fresh green pastures;
  And may thy lustrous crescent grow a honeymoon
    for me!
Come merry month of the cuckoo and the violet!
  Come weeping Loveliness in all thy blue delight!
Lo! the nest is ready, let me not languish longer!
  Bring her to my arms on the first May night.

GEORGE MEREDITH

THE OWL AND THE PUSSY-CAT

The Owl and the Pussy-Cat went to sea
    In a beautiful pea-green boat.
They took some honey, and plenty of money
    Wrapped up in a five-pound note.
The Owl looked up to the stars above,
    And sang to a small guitar,
'O lovely Pussy! O Pussy, my love,
What a beautiful Pussy you are,
            You are,
            You are!
What a beautiful Pussy you are!'

Pussy said to the Owl, 'You elegant fowl!
    How charmingly sweet you sing!
O let us be married! too long we have tarried:
    But what shall we do for a ring?'
They sailed away, for a year and a day,
    To the land where the Bong-Tree grows,
And there in a wood a Piggy-wig stood,
With a ring at the end of his nose,
            His nose,
            His nose!
With a ring at the end of his nose.

'Dear Pig, are you willing to sell for one shilling
　　Your ring?' Said the Piggy, 'I will.'
So they took it away, and were married next day
　　By the Turkey who lives on the hill.
They dinèd on mince, and slices of quince,
　　Which they ate with a runcible spoon;
And hand in hand, on the edge of the sand
　　They danced by the light of the moon,
　　　　The moon,
　　　　The moon,
They danced by the light of the moon.

MY LAST DUCHESS

FERRARA

That's my last Duchess painted on the wall,
Looking as if she were alive. I call
That piece a wonder, now: Frà Pandolf's hands
Worked busily a day, and there she stands.
Will't please you sit and look at her? I said
'Frà Pandolf' by design, for never read
Strangers like you that pictured countenance,
The depth and passion of its earnest glance,
But to myself they turned (since none puts by
The curtain I have drawn for you, but I)
And seemed as they would ask me, if they durst,
How such a glance came there; so, not the first
Are you to turn and ask thus. Sir, 'twas not
Her husband's presence only, called that spot
Of joy into the Duchess' cheek: perhaps
Frà Pandolf chanced to say 'Her mantle laps
Over my lady's wrist too much,' or 'Paint
Must never hope to reproduce the faint
Half-flush that dies along her throat': such stuff
Was courtesy, she thought, and cause enough
For calling up that spot of joy. She had
A heart – how shall I say? – too soon made glad,
Too easily impressed; she liked whate'er
She looked on, and her looks went everywhere.

Sir, 'twas all one! My favour at her breast,
The dropping of the daylight in the West,
The bough of cherries some officious fool
Broke in the orchard for her, the white mule
She rode with round the terrace – all and each
Would draw from her alike the approving speech,
Or blush, at least. She thanked men, – good! but
    thanked
Somehow – I know not how – as if she ranked
My gift of a nine-hundred-years-old name
With anybody's gift. Who'd stoop to blame
This sort of trifling? Even had you skill
In speech – (which I have not) – to make your will
Quite clear to such an one, and say, 'Just this
Or that in you disgusts me; here you miss,
Or there exceed the mark' – and if she let
Herself be lessoned so, nor plainly set
Her wits to yours, forsooth, and made excuse,
– E'en then would be some stooping; and I choose
Never to stoop. Oh sir, she smiled, no doubt,
Whene'er I passed her; but who passed without
Much the same smile? This grew; I gave commands;
Then all smiles stopped together. There she stands
As if alive. Will't please you rise? We'll meet
The company below, then. I repeat,
The Count your master's known munificence
Is ample warrant that no just pretence

Of mine for dowry will be disallowed;
Though his fair daughter's self, as I avowed
At starting, is my object. Nay, we'll go
Together down, sir. Notice Neptune, though,
Taming a sea-horse, thought a rarity,
Which Claus of Innsbruck cast in bronze for me!

THE BETROTHAL

Oh, come, my lad, or go, my lad,
And love me if you like.
I shall not hear the door shut
Nor the knocker strike.

Oh, bring me gifts or beg me gifts,
And wed me if you will.
I'd make a man a good wife,
Sensible and still.

And why should I be cold, my lad,
And why should you repine,
Because I love a dark head
That never will be mine?

I might as well be easing you
As lie alone in bed
And waste the night in wanting
A cruel dark head.

You might as well be calling yours
What never will be his,
And one of us be happy.
There's few enough as is.

WEDDINGS

And may her bridegroom bring her to a house
Where all's accustomed, ceremonious;
For arrogance and hatred are the wares
Peddled in the thoroughfares.
How but in custom and in ceremony
Are innocence and beauty born?
Ceremony's a name for the rich horn,
And custom for the spreading laurel tree.

W. B. YEATS

MARRIAGE MORNING

Light, so low upon earth,
    You send a flash to the sun.
Here is the golden close of love,
    All my wooing is done.
Oh, the woods and the meadows,
    Woods, where we hid from the wet,
Stiles where we stayed to be kind,
    Meadows in which we met!
Light, so low in the vale
    You flash and lighten afar,
For this is the golden morning of love,
    And you are his morning star.
Flash, I am coming, I come,
    By meadow and stile and wood,
Oh, lighten into my eyes and my heart,
    Into my heart and my blood!
Heart, are you great enough
    For a love that never tires?
O heart, are you great enough for love?
    I have heard of thorns and briers.
Over the thorns and briers,
    Over the meadows and stiles,
Over the world to the end of it
    Flash for a million miles.

ALFRED, LORD TENNYSON

WEDDING MORN

The morning breaks like a pomegranate
    In a shining crack of red;
Ah, when to-morrow the dawn comes late
    Whitening across the bed
It will find me watching at the marriage gate
    And waiting while light is shed
On him who is sleeping satiate
    With a sunk, unconscious head.

And when the dawn comes creeping in,
    Cautiously I shall raise
Myself to watch the daylight win
    On my first of days,
As it shows him sleeping a sleep he got
    With me, as under my gaze
He grows distinct, and I see his hot
    Face freed of the wavering blaze.

Then I shall know which image of God
    My man is made toward;
And I shall see my sleeping rod
    Or my life's reward;
And I shall count the stamp and worth
    Of the man I've accepted as mine,
Shall see an image of heaven or of earth
    On his minted metal shine.

Oh, and I long to see him sleep
    In my power utterly;
So I shall know what I have to keep. . . .
    I long to see
My love, that spinning coin, laid still
    And plain at the side of me
For me to reckon – for surely he will
    Be wealth of life to me.

And then he will be mine, he will lie
    Revealed to me;
Patent and open beneath my eye
    He will sleep of me;
He will lie negligent, resign
    His truth to me, and I
Shall watch the dawn light up for me
    This fate of mine.

And as I watch the wan light shine
    On his sleep that is filled of me,
On his brow where the curved wisps clot and twine
    Carelessly,
On his lips where the light breaths come and go
    Unconsciously,
On his limbs in sleep at last laid low
    Helplessly,
I shall weep, oh I shall weep, I know
    For joy or for misery.

D. H. LAWRENCE

THE WEDDING MORNING

Tabitha dressed for her wedding: –
'Tabby, why look so sad?'
' – O I feel a great gloominess spreading, spreading,
Instead of supremely glad! . . .

'I called on Carry last night,
And he came whilst I was there,
Not knowing I'd called. So I kept out of sight,
And I heard what he said to her:

' " – Ah, I'd far liefer marry
You, Dear, to-morrow!" he said,
"But that cannot be." – O I'd give him to Carry,
And willingly see them wed,

'But how can I do it when
His baby will soon be born?
After that I hope I may die. And then
She can have him. I shall not mourn!'

THE BRIDE SINGS

My beloved is mine, and I am his: he feedeth among
the lilies.

Until the day break and the shadows flee away, turn,
my beloved, and be thou like a roe or a young hart
upon the mountains of Bether.

By night I sought him whom my soul loveth: I sought
him but I found him not.

I will rise now and go about the city in the streets, and
in the broad ways I will seek him whom my soul
loveth: I sought him but I found him not.

The watchmen that go about the city found me: to
whom I said, Saw ye him whom my soul loveth?

It was but a little that I passed from them, but I found
him whom my soul loveth: I held him and would
not let him go, until I had brought him into my
mother's house, and into the chamber of her that
conceived me.

THE BRIDE

Call to me, love, call to me loudly!
Don't let your bride stand so long at the window.
In the old shaded plane-tree avenues
the evening no longer wakes:
they are empty.

And if you don't come and lock me up with your voice
in the deep nocturnal house,
then I must pour myself out of my hands
into the gardens of
dark blue . . .

THE MARRIAGE OF HERO AND LEANDER

They had a wedding, but no Dancing there
A Bride-bed, but they did no singing heare;
Their sacred Nuptials no Poet prais'd,
About their private bed no Torches blaz'd,
No Dancer in a nimble caper sprung,
No Hymnes the Father or grave Mother sung.
But Darkness at Love's houres the Bride-bed made,
Drest up the Room: the Bride's Veyle was the shade.
Farre from Epithalamions were they matcht;
Night only at their ceremonies watcht;
Aurora never did Leander view
A Bride-groome, in that bed he so well knew.
Who swam back to Abydos, breathing still
Those Hymeneall Sweetes that never fill.
But long-veyl'd Hero mock't her Parents sight,
A virgin all the day, a Wife by night;
Both often chid the Morning to the West,
And thus the fury of their loves supprest,
Enjoying secret, but short-liv'd delights,
For short time dates their strange stoln marriage-rites.

MUSAEUS   45

TRANSLATED BY ROBERT STAPYLTON

LORD THOMAS AND FAIR ELEANOR

Lord Thomas he was a bold forester,
　　And a chaser of the king's deer;
Fair Eleanor was a fine woman,
　　And Lord Thomas loved her dear.

'Come, riddle my riddle, dear mother,' he said,
　　'And riddle us both in one;
Whether I shall marry with sweet Eleanor,
　　And let the brown girl alone?'

'The brown girl she has got houses and land,
　　Fair Eleanor she has got none;
Therefore, I charge thee on my blessing,
　　Bring me the brown girl home.'

And as it befel on a holiday,
　　As many more do beside,
Lord Thomas went to fair Eleanor,
　　That should have been his bride.

'What news, what news, Lord Thomas?' she said,
　　'What news hast thou brought to me?'
'I am come to bid thee to my wedding,
　　And that's sad news for thee.'

'O, God forbid! Lord Thomas,' she said,
    'That such a thing should ever be done;
I thought to have been thy bride myself,
    And thou been the bridegroom.'

She clothed herself in gallant attire,
    And her merry men in green;
And as she rode through every place,
    They took her to be some queen.

When she came to Lord Thomas's gate,
    She knocked at the ring;
And who was so ready as Lord Thomas,
    To let fair Eleanor in.

'Is this your bride?' fair Eleanor said,
    'Methinks she looks wondrous brown;
Thou might'st have had as fair a woman,
    As ever trod upon the ground.'

'Despise her not,' Lord Thomas he said,
    'Despise her not unto me;
For better I love thy little finger,
    Than all her whole body.'

This brown girl had a little penknife,
　　Which was both keen and sharp,
And betwixt the short ribs and the long,
　　She prick'd fair Eleanor to the heart.

'O Christ, now save me,' Lord Thomas he said,
　　'Methinks thou looks wondrous wan;
Thou us'd to look as good a colour,
　　As ever the sun shone on.'

'O art thou blind, Lord Thomas?' she said,
　　'Or canst thou not very well see;
O, dost thou not see my own heart's blood,
　　Runs trickling down my knee.'

Lord Thomas he had a sword by his side,
　　As he walked about the hall;
He cut his bride's head from her shoulders,
　　And flung it against the wall.

He set his sword upon the ground,
　　And the point against his heart;
There never was three lovers, sure,
　　That sooner did depart.

THE FROG AND THE MOUSE

A frog went walking one fine day
        A-hmmm, A-hmmm,
A frog went walking one fine day,
He met Miss Mousie on the way
        A-hmmm, A-hmmm.

He said Miss Mousie will you marry me,
        A-hmmm, A-hmmm,
He said Miss Mousie will you marry me,
We'll live together in a hollow tree,
        A-hmmm, A-hmmm.

The first to the wedding was farmer Brown
        A-hmmm, A-hmmm,
The first to the wedding was farmer Brown
He brought his wife in a wedding gown.
        A-hmmm, A-hmmm.

The second to the wedding was Dr. Dick
        A-hmmm, A-hmmm,
The second to the wedding was Dr. Dick
He ate so much that he nearly got sick.
        A-hmmm, A-hmmm.

The third to the wedding was Grandma Green
      A-hmmm, A-hmmm,
The third to the wedding was Grandma Green
Her shawl was blue but it wasn't clean.
      A-hmmm, A-hmmm.

And what do you think they had for supper?
      A-hmmm, A-hmmm,
And what do you think they had for supper?
Some fried mosquitoes without any butter.
      A-hmmm, A-hmmm.

And what do you think they had for a fiddle?
      A-hmmm, A-hmmm,
And what do you think they had for a fiddle?
An old tin can with a hole in the middle,
      A-hmmm, A-hmmm.

And what do you think they had on the shelf?
      A-hmmm, A-hmmm,
And what do you think they had on the shelf?
If you want to find out, go look for yourself!
      A-hmmm, A-hmmm.

CEREMONIALS

RAISING OF THE BRIDEGROOM

Though it be some divorce to think of you
    Singly, so much one are you two,
    Yet let me here contemplate thee,
First, cheerful Bridegroom, and first let me see,
    How thou prevent'st the sun,
And his red foaming horses dost outrun,
How having laid down in thy Sovereign's breast
All businesses, from thence to reinvest
Them, when these triumphs cease, thou forward art
To show to her, who doth the like impart,
The fire of thy inflaming eyes, and of thy loving heart.

RAISING OF THE BRIDE

But now, to thee, fair Bride, it is some wrong,
    To think thou wert in bed so long,
    Since soon thou liest down first, 'tis fit
Thou in first rising shouldst allow for it.
    Powder thy radiant hair,
Which if without such ashes thou wouldst wear,
Thou, which to all which come to look upon,
Art meant for Phoebus, wouldst be Phaëton.
For our ease, give thine eyes th' unusual part
Of joy, a tear; so quenched, thou mayst impart,
To us that come, thy inflaming eyes, to him,
        thy loving heart.

HER APPARELLING

Thus thou descend'st to our infirmity,
Who can the sun in water see.
So dost thou, when in silk and gold,
Thou cloud'st thyself; since we which do behold,
Are dust, and worms, 'tis just
Our objects be the fruits of worms and dust;
Let every jewel be a glorious star,
Yet stars are not so pure, as their spheres are.
And though thou stoop, to appear to us in part,
Still in that picture thou entirely art,
Which thy inflaming eyes have made within his
loving heart...

FEASTS AND REVELS

But you are over-blessed. Plenty this day
Injures; it causeth time to stay;
The tables groan, as though this feast
Would, as the flood, destroy all fowl and beast.
And were the doctrine new
That the earth moved, this day would make it true;
For every part to dance and revel goes.
They tread the air, and fall not where they rose.
Though six hours since, the sun to bed did part,
The masks and banquets will not yet impart
A sunset to these weary eyes, a centre to this heart.

THE BRIDE'S GOING TO BED

What mean'st thou, Bride, this company to keep?
  To sit up, till thou fain wouldst sleep?
  Thou mayst not, when thou art laid, do so.
Thyself must to him a new banquet grow,
  And you must entertain
And do all this day's dances o'er again.
Know that if sun and moon together do
Rise in one point, they do not set so too.
Therefore thou mayst, fair Bride, to bed depart,
Thou art not gone, being gone, where e'er thou art,
Thou leav'st in him thy watchful eyes, in him thy
    loving heart.

THE BRIDEGROOM'S COMING

As he that sees a star fall, runs apace,
  And finds a jelly in the place,
  So doth the Bridegroom haste as much,
Being told this star is fall'n, and finds her such.
  And as friends may look strange,
By a new fashion, or apparel's change,
Their souls, though long acquainted they had been,
These clothes, their bodies, never yet had seen.
Therefore at first she modestly might start,
But must forthwith surrender every part,
As freely, as each to each before, gave either eye
    or heart.

JOHN DONNE   53

HIAWATHA'S WEDDING-FEAST

Sumptuous was the feast Nokomis
Made at Hiawatha's wedding;
All the bowls were made of bass-wood,
White and polished very smoothly,
All the spoons of horn of bison,
Black and polished very smoothly.

She had sent through all the village
Messengers with wands of willow,
As a sign of invitation,
As a token of the feasting;
And the wedding guests assembled,
Clad in all their richest raiment,
Robes of fur and belts of wampum,
Splendid with their paint and plumage,
Beautiful with beads and tassels.

First they ate the sturgeon, Nahma,
And the pike, the Maskenozha,
Caught and cooked by old Nokomis;
Then on pemican they feasted,
Pemican and buffalo marrow,
Haunch of deer and hump of bison,
Yellow cakes of the Mondamin,
And the wild rice of the river.

But the gracious Hiawatha,
And the lovely Laughing Water,

And the careful old Nokomis,
Tasted not the food before them,
Only waited on the others,
Only served their guests in silence.
    And when all the guests had finished,
Old Nokomis, brisk and busy,
From an ample pouch of otter,
Filled the red-stone pipes for smoking
With tobacco from the South-land,
Mixed with bark of the red willow,
And with herbs and leaves of fragrance.

A WEDDING OUT WEST

I saw the marriage of the trapper in the open air in the
      far west, the bride was a red girl,
Her father and his friends sat near cross-legged and
      dumbly smoking, they had moccasins to their feet
      and large thick blankets hanging from their
      shoulders,
On a bank lounged the trapper, he was drest mostly in
      skins, his luxuriant beard and curls protected his
      neck, he held his bride by the hand,
She had long eyelashes, her head was bare, her coarse
      straight locks descended upon her voluptuous
      limbs and reach'd to her feet.

ON THE MARRIAGE OF A VIRGIN

Walking alone in a multitude of loves when morning's
    light
Surprised in the opening of her nightlong eyes
His golden yesterday asleep upon the iris
And this day's sun leapt up the sky out of her thighs
Was miraculous virginity old as loaves and fishes,
Though the moment of a miracle is unending lightning
And the shipyards of Galilee's footprints hide a navy
    of doves.

No longer will the vibrations of the sun desire on
Her deepsea pillow where once she married alone,
Her heart all ears and eyes, lips catching the avalanche
Of the golden ghost who ringed with his streams her
    mercury bone,
Who under the lids of her windows hoisted his golden
    luggage,
For a man sleeps when fire leapt down and she learns
    through his arm
That other sun, the jealous coursing of the unrivalled
    blood.

AT THE ALTAR-RAIL

'My bride is not coming, alas!' says the groom,
And the telegram shakes in his hand. 'I own
It was hurried! We met at a dancing-room
When I went to the Cattle-Show alone,
And then, next night, where the Fountain leaps,
And the Street of the Quarter-Circle sweeps.

'Ay, she won me to ask her to be my wife –
'Twas foolish perhaps! – to forsake the ways
Of the flaring town for a farmer's life.
She agreed. And we fixed it. Now she says:
"It's sweet of you, dear, to prepare me a nest,
But a swift, short, gay life suits me best.
What I really am you have never gleaned;
I had eaten the apple ere you were weaned." '

FOR A REMARRIAGE
(OF CATO AND MARCIA)

No garlands on the marriage doores were worne,
Nor linnen fillets did the posts adorne:
No bridall Tapers shone: no bed on high
With Ivory steps, and gold embrodery:
No Matron in a towred crowne, that led
The Bride, forbid her on the threshold tread:
No yellow veile cover'd her face, to hide
The fearefull blushes of a modest Bride:
No precious girdle guirded her loose Gowne:
No Chaine adornd her necke; nor linnen downe
From off her shoulders her nak'd armes orespred;
So as she was, funerall habited,
Even like her Sonnes, her Husband she embrac'd,
A funerall Robe above her purple plac'd.
The usual Jests were spar'd: the husband wants,
After the Sabine use, his marriage tants.
None of their kindred met; the knot they tye
Silent: content with Brutus auspicie.

LUCAN

TRANSLATED BY TOM MAY

UPON A SECOND MARRIAGE
for H. I. P.

Orchards, we linger here because
Women we love stand propped in your green prisons,
Obedient to such justly bending laws
      Each one longs to take root,
  Lives to confess whatever season's
Pride of blossom or endeavor's fruit
  May to her rustling boughs have risen.

  Then autumn reddens the whole mind.
No more, she vows, the dazzle of a year
Shall woo her from your bare cage of loud wind,
      Promise the ring and run
  To burn the altar, reappear
With apple blossoms for the credulous one.
  Orchards, we wonder that we linger here!

Orchards we planted, trees we shook
To learn what you were bearing, say we stayed
Because one winter dusk we half-mistook
      Frost on a bleakened bough
  For blossoms, and were half-afraid
To miss the old persuasion, should we go.
  And spring did come, and discourse made

Enough of weddings to us all
That, loving her for whom the whole world grows
Fragrant and white, we linger to recall
    As down aisles of cut trees
  How a tall trunk's cross-section shows
Concentric rings, those many marriages
    That life on each live thing bestows.

ON THE TWO DWARFS THAT
WERE MARRIED AT COURT

Design, or chance, makes others wive;
But nature did this match contrive;
Eve might as well have Adam fled,
As she denied her little bed
To him, for whom Heaven seemed to frame,
And measure out, this only dame.
   Thrice happy is that humble pair,
Beneath the level of all care!
Over whose heads those arrows fly
Of sad distrust and jealousy;
Secured in as high extreme,
As if the world held none but them.
   To him the fairest nymphs do show
Like moving mountains, topped with snow;
And every man a Polypheme
Does to his Galatea seem;
None may presume her faith to prove;
He proffers death that proffers love.
   Ah, Chloris, that kind Nature thus
From all the world had severed us;
Creating for ourselves us two,
As love has me for only you!

EPITHALAMIUM ON A LATE HAPPY MARRIAGE

When *Hymen* once the mutual Bands has wove,
Exchanging Heart for Heart, and Love for Love,
The happy Pair, with mutual Bliss elate,
Own to be single's an imperfect State.
But when two Hearts united thus agree
With equal sense, and equal Constancy,
This, HAPPINESS, is thy extreamest Goal,
'Tis Marriage both of Body, and of Soul,
'Tis making Heav'n below with matchless Love,
And's a fair Step to reach the Heav'n above.

CHRISTOPHER SMART   63

TO A FRIEND ON HIS NUPTIALS

When Jove lay blest in his Alcmæna's charms,
Three nights, in one, he prest her in his arms;
The sun lay set, and conscious nature strove
To shade her god, and to prolong his love.
    From that auspicious night Alcides* came,
What less could rise from Jove, and such a dame?
    May this auspicious night with that compare,
Nor less the joys, nor less the rising heir;
He strong as Jove, she like Alcmæna fair!

*Hercules

A WEDDING TOAST
M. C. H.   C. H. W.
14 July 1971

St. John tells how, at Cana's wedding-feast,
The water-pots poured wine in such amount
That by his sober count
There were a hundred gallons at the least.

It made no earthly sense, unless to show
How whatsoever love elects to bless
Brims to a sweet excess
That can without depletion overflow.

Which is to say that what love sees is true;
That the world's fullness is not made but found.
Life hungers to abound
And pour its plenty out for such as you.

Now, if your loves will lend an ear to mine,
I toast you both, good son and dear new daughter.
May you not lack for water,
And may that water smack of Cana's wine.

WEDDING NIGHT

Now night is come, now soon her disarray,
And in her bed her lay;
Lay her in lilies and in violets,
And silken curtains over her display,
And odoured sheets, and Arras coverlets.
Behold how goodly my fair love does lie
In proud humility;
Like unto Maia, when as Jove her took,
In Tempe, lying on the flowery grass,
'Twixt sleep and wake, after she weary was,
With bathing in the Acidalian brook.
Now it is night, ye damsels may be gone,
And leave my love alone,
And leave likewise your former lay to sing;
The woods no more shall answer, nor your echo ring.

Now welcome, night, thou night so long expected,
That long day's labour dost at last defray,
And all my cares, which cruel love collected,
Hast summed in one, and cancelled for aye:
Spread thy broad wing over my love and me,
That no man may us see,
And in thy sable mantle us enwrap,
From fear of peril and foul horror free.
Let no false treason seek us to entrap,

Nor any dread disquiet once annoy
The safety of our joy:
But let the night be calm and quietsome,
Without tempestuous storms or sad affray;
Like as when Jove with fair Alcmena lay,
When he begot the great Tirynthian groom;
Or like as when he with thyself did lie,
And begot majesty.
And let the maids and young men cease to sing;
Ne let the woods them answer, nor their echo ring.

Let no lamenting cries, nor doleful tears,
Be heard all night within nor yet without;
Ne let false whispers, breeding hidden fears,
Break gentle sleep with misconceived doubt.
Let no deluding dreams nor dreadful sights
Make sudden sad affrights;
Ne let housefires, nor lightning's helpless harms,
Ne let the Puck, nor other evil sprights,
Ne let mischievous witches with their charms,
Ne let hobgoblins, names whose sense we see not,
Fray us with things that be not.
Let not the screech owl, nor the stork be heard;
Nor the night raven that still deadly yells,
Nor damned ghosts called up with mighty spells,
Nor grisly vultures make us once affeared:
Ne let th' unpleasant quire of frogs still croaking

Make us to wish their choking.
Let none of these their dreary accents sing;
Ne let the woods them answer, nor their echo ring.

But let still silence true night watches keep,
That sacred peace may in assurance reign,
And timely sleep, when it is time to sleep,
May pour his limbs forth on your pleasant plain,
The whiles an hundred little winged loves,
Like divers feathered doves,
Shall fly and flutter round about your bed,
And in the secret dark, that none reproves,
Their pretty stealths shall work, and snares shall
    spread
To filch away sweet snatches of delight,
Concealed through covert night.
Ye sons of Venus, play your sports at will,
For greedy pleasure, careless of your toys,
Thinks more upon her paradise of joys,
Than what ye do, albeit good or ill.
All night therefore attend your merry play,
For it will soon be day:
Now none doth hinder you, that say or sing;
Ne will the woods now answer, nor your echo ring ...

A BEAUTY'S SOLILOQUY
DURING HER HONEYMOON

Too late, too late! I did not know my fairness
    Would catch the world's keen eyes so!
How the men look at me! My radiant rareness
    I deemed not they would prize so!

That I was a peach for any man's possession
    Why did not some one say
Before I leased myself in an hour's obsession
    To this dull mate for aye!

His days are mine. I am one who cannot steal her
    Ahead of his plodding pace:
As he is, so am I. One doomed to feel her
    A wasted form and face!

I was so blind! It did sometimes just strike me
    All girls were not as I,
But, dwelling much alone, how few were like me
    I could not well descry;

Till, at this Grand Hotel, all looks bend on me
    In homage as I pass
To take my seat at breakfast, dinner, – con me
    As poorly spoused, alas!

I was too young. I dwelt too much on duty:
    If I had guessed my powers
Where might have sailed this cargo of choice beauty
    In its unanchored hours!

Well, husband, poor plain man; I've lost life's battle! –
    Come – let them look at me.
O damn, don't show in your looks that I'm your chattel
    Quite so emphatically!

In a London Hotel, 1892

HARMONY

Long may this happy heaven tyed band
   exercise its most holy art,
keeping her heart within his hand
   keeping his hand upon her heart;
     but from her eyes
       feele he noe Charmes,
      finde she noe joy
       but in his armes;
May each maintaine a well fledged neast
of winged loves in eithers breast
Be each of them a mutuall sacrefice
       of eithers eyes:

May their whole life a sweet song prove
   sett to two well composed parts,
by musickes noblest master, Love,
   playd on the strings of both their harts;
     whose mutuall sound
       may ever meete
     in a just round,
       not short though sweet;
Long may heaven listen to the songe,
and thinke it short though it bee long;
oh prove't a well sett song indeed, which showes
       sweet'st in the Close.

SONG

Now hath *Flora* rob'd her bowers
To befrend this place with flowers:
    Strowe aboute, strowe aboute.
The Skye rayn'd neuer kindlyer Showers.
Flowers with Bridalls well agree,
Fresh as Brides, and Bridegromes be:
    Strowe aboute, strowe aboute;
And mixe them with fit melodie.
    Earth hath no Princelier flowers
Than Roses white, and Roses red,
But they must still be mingled:
And as a Rose new pluckt from *Venus* thorne,
So doth a Bride her Bride-groomes bed adorne.

Diuers diuers Flowers affect
For some priuate deare respect:
   Strowe about, strowe about.
Let euery one his owne protect;
But hees none of *Floras* friend
That will not the Rose commend.
   Strow about, strow about;
Let Princes Princely flowers defend:
   Roses, the Gardens pride,
Are flowers for loue and flowers for Kinges,
In courts desir'd and Weddings:
And as a Rose in *Venus* bosome worne,
So doth a Bridegroome his Brides bed adorne.

WEDDING-WIND

The wind blew all my wedding-day,
And my wedding-night was the night of the high wind;
And a stable door was banging, again and again,
That he must go and shut it, leaving me
Stupid in candlelight, hearing rain,
Seeing my face in the twisted candlestick,
Yet seeing nothing. When he came back
He said the horses were restless, and I was sad
That any man or beast that night should lack
The happiness I had.

           Now in the day
All's ravelled under the sun by the wind's blowing.
He has gone to look at the floods, and I
Carry a chipped pail to the chicken-run,
Set it down, and stare. All is the wind
Hunting through clouds and forests, thrashing
My apron and the hanging cloths on the line.
Can it be borne, this bodying-forth by wind
Of joy my actions turn on, like a thread
Carrying beads? Shall I be let to sleep
Now this perpetual morning shares my bed?
Can even death dry up
These new delighted lakes, conclude
Our kneeling as cattle by all-generous waters?

DOMESTICITIES

The ring, so worn as you behold,
So thin, so pale, is yet of gold:
The passion such it was to prove –
Worn with life's care, love yet was love.

GEORGE CRABBE

COUPLE
(*for* Isabel Archer)

You turn to the window, and whatever it was
we were discussing escapes
in a flutter of poplar leaves:
we are left with mere afternoon, in a daze,

aging, but still taking notes, while
the fritillary summer flaps
from the laundry line, and bell tolls blossom
in air, floating in from the tawniest hill.

I boiled months
of sunlight, trapped them in jars
of apricot jam. Where were
you last night, where was I? Who counts

the slashes? We take
our time. This life
in the villa continues
behind high glass-fringed walls, smoke

drifting in from the fields, letters
arriving torn, Antiquity
more legible than our own
dear pasts. With gin and bitters

and years, we'll understand, how comprehensible
our magics will have become, how tuned
to our garden where such lush symbols thrive.
We'll be a story, we'll be able

to parse it alone in crepuscular light,
so pleased, hearing distant bleats of horns
from every blind loop of the road as small
cars accelerate into the future, trusting not

to collide, each with its destined mate.

EROS TURANNOS

She fears him, and will always ask
   What fated her to choose him;
She meets in his engaging mask
   All reasons to refuse him;
But what she meets and what she fears
Are less than are the downward years,
Drawn slowly to the foamless weirs
   Of age, were she to lose him.

Between a blurred sagacity
   That once had power to sound him,
And Love, that will not let him be
   The Judas that she found him,
Her pride assuages her almost,
As if it were alone the cost. –
He sees that he will not be lost,
   And waits and looks around him.

A sense of ocean and old trees
   Envelops and allures him;
Tradition, touching all he sees,
   Beguiles and reassures him;
And all her doubts of what he says
Are dimmed with what she knows of days –
Till even prejudice delays
   And fades, and she secures him.

The falling leaf inaugurates
    The reign of her confusion;
The pounding wave reverberates
    The dirge of her illusion;
And home, where passion lived and died,
Becomes a place where she can hide,
While all the town and harbor side
    Vibrate with her seclusion.

We tell you, tapping on our brows,
    The story as it should be, –
As if the story of a house
    Were told, or ever could be;
We'll have no kindly veil between
Her visions and those we have seen, –
As if we guessed what hers have been,
    Or what they are or would be.

Meanwhile we do no harm; for they
    That with a god have striven,
Not hearing much of what we say,
    Take what the god has given;
Though like waves breaking it may be,
Or like a changed familiar tree,
Or like a stairway to the sea
    Where down the blind are driven.

FOR POORER

'Give me that bit of rag; or take the boy
And try to keep him warm.' 'The ground this side
Is bare, and there's at least some straw at yours.'
The burglar who had quietly entered heard,
Threw over them the ragged cloak he'd lifted
Elsewhere, and crept away again, in tears.

ANONYMOUS, SANSKRIT
TRANSLATED BY JOHN BROUGH

AT THE DINNER-TABLE

I sat at dinner in my prime,
And glimpsed my face in the sideboard-glass,
And started as if I had seen a crime,
And prayed the ghastly show might pass.

Wrenched wrinkled features met my sight,
Grinning back to me as my own;
I well-nigh fainted with affright
At finding me a haggard crone.

My husband laughed. He had slily set
A warping mirror there, in whim
To startle me. My eyes grew wet;
I spoke not all the eve to him.

He was sorry, he said, for what he had done,
And took away the distorting glass,
Uncovering the accustomed one;
And so it ended? No, alas,

Fifty years later, when he died,
I sat me in the selfsame chair,
Thinking of him. Till, weary-eyed,
I saw the sideboard facing there;

And from its mirror looked the lean
Thing I'd become, each wrinkle and score
The image of me that I had seen
In jest there fifty years before.

A QUESTION OF MARRIAGE

'I yield you my whole heart, Countess,' said he;
'Come, Dear, and be queen of my studio.'
'No, sculptor. You're merely my friend,' said she:
'We dine our artists; but marry them – no.'

'Be it thus,' he replied. And his love, so strong,
He subdued as a stoic should. Anon
He wived some damsel who'd loved him long,
Of lineage noteless; and chiselled on.

And a score years passed. As a master-mind
The world made much of his marching fame,
And his wife's little charms, with his own entwined,
Won day after day increased acclaim.

The countess-widow had closed with a mate
In rank and wealth of her own degree,
And they moved among the obscurely great
Of an order that had no novelty.

And oldening – neither with blame nor praise –
Their stately lives begot no stir,
And she saw that when death should efface her days
All men would abandon thought of her;

And said to herself full gloomily:
'Far better for me had it been to shine
The wench of a genius such as he
Than rust as the wife of a spouse like mine!'

THE PAINTER'S WIFE

She was tangled up in her own self-conceit, a woman,
and her passion could only flare through the meshes
towards other women, in communion;
the presence of a man made her recoil
and burn blue and cold, like the flame in a miner's lamp
when the after-damp is around it.

Yet she seemed to know nothing about it
and devoted herself to her husband
and made him paint her nude, time after time,
and each time it came out the same, a horrible sexless,
        lifeless abstraction
of the female form, technically 'beautiful', actually
        a white machine-drawing, more null than death.

And she was so pleased with it, she thought one day
        it would be recognised as 'great'.
And he thought so too.
Nobody else did.

THE MARRIAGE

I look at the nude woman,
With the little head
And with the galumphing thighs
And with the manly feet,
And I turn to the artist
And I ask him
Whatever brought him
To dream up such a thing on canvas,
He strikes a match
And stuffs the pipe into his mouth
And answers. –
It just turns out that
He – *puff.*
Himself – *puff.*
Was married to her – *puff.*
In Paris, indeed – *puff.*

MOISHE LEIB HALPERN
TRANSLATED BY JOHN HOLLANDER

UPON ONE LILLIE, WHO MARRIED WITH A MAID CALL'D ROSE

What times of sweetnesse this faire day fore-shows,
When as the Lilly married with the Rose!
What next is lookt for? but we all sho'd see
To spring from these a sweet Posterity.

THE STORY OF BAUCIS AND PHILEMON

                    An oak-tree stands
Beside a linden, in the Phrygian hills.
There's a low wall around them. I have seen
The place myself; a prince once sent me there
To land ruled by his father. Not far off
A great marsh lies, once habitable land,
But now a playground full of coots and divers.
Jupiter came here, once upon a time,
Disguised as mortal man, and Mercury,
His son, came with him, having laid aside
Both wand and wings. They tried a thousand houses,
Looking for rest; they found a thousand houses
Shut in their face. But one at last received them,
A humble cottage, thatched with straw and reeds.
A good old woman, Baucis, and her husband,
A good old man, Philemon, used to live there.
They had married young, they had grown old together
In the same cottage; they were very poor,
But faced their poverty with cheerful spirit
And made its burden light by not complaining.
It would do you little good to ask for servants
Or masters in that household, for the couple
Were all the house; both gave and followed orders.
So, when the gods came to this little cottage,
Ducking their heads to enter, the old man

Pulled out a rustic bench for them to rest on,
As Baucis spread a homespun cover for it.
And then she poked the ashes around a little,
Still warm from last night's fire, and got them going
With leaves and bark, and blew at them a little,
Without much breath to spare, and added kindling,
The wood split fine, and the dry twigs, made smaller
By breaking them over the knee, and put them under
A copper kettle, and then she took the cabbage
Her man had brought from the well-watered garden,
And stripped the outer leaves off. And Philemon
Reached up, with a forked stick, for the side of bacon,
That hung below the smoky beam, and cut it,
Saved up so long, a fair-sized chunk, and dumped it
In the boiling water. They made conversation
To keep the time from being too long, and brought
A couch with willow frame and feet, and on it
They put a sedge-grass mattress, and above it
Such drapery as they had, and did not use
Except on great occasions. Even so,
It was pretty worn, it had only cost a little
When purchased new, but it went well enough
With a willow couch. And so the gods reclined.
Baucis, her skirts tucked up, was setting the table
With trembling hands. One table-leg was wobbly;
A piece of shell fixed that. She scoured the table,
Made level now, with a handful of green mint,

Put on the olives, black or green, and cherries
Preserved in dregs of wine, endive and radish,
And cottage cheese, and eggs, turned over lightly
In the warm ash, with shells unbroken. The dishes,
Of course, were earthenware, and the mixing-bowl
For wine was the same silver, and the goblets
Were beech, the inside coated with yellow wax.
No time at all, and the warm food was ready,
And wine brought out, of no particular vintage,
And pretty soon they had to clear the table
For the second course: here there were nuts and figs
And dates and plums and apples in wide baskets –
Remember how apples smell? – and purple grapes
Fresh from the vines, and a white honeycomb
As centerpiece, and all around the table
Shone kindly faces, nothing mean or poor
Or skimpy in good will.

              The mixing-bowl,
As often as it was drained, kept filling up
All by itself, and the wine was never lower.
And this was strange, and scared them when they saw it.
They raised their hands and prayed, a little shaky –
'Forgive us, please, our lack of preparation,
Our meagre fare!' They had one goose, a guardian,
Watchdog, he might be called, of their estate,
And now decided they had better kill him
To make their offering better. But the goose

Was swift of wing, too swift for slow old people
To catch, and they were weary from the effort,
And could not catch the bird, who fled for refuge,
Or so it seemed, to the presence of the strangers.
'Don't kill him,' said the gods, and then continued:
'We are gods, you know: this wicked neighborhood
Will pay as it deserves to; do not worry,
You will not be hurt, but leave the house, come with us,
Both of you, to the mountain-top!' Obeying,
With staff and cane, they made the long climb, slowly
And painfully, and rested, where a bowman
Could reach the top with a long shot, looked down,
Saw water everywhere, only their cottage
Standing above the flood. And while they wondered
And wept a little for their neighbors' trouble,
The house they used to live in, the poor quarters
Small for the two of them, became a temple:
Forked wooden props turned into marble columns;
The thatch grew brighter yellow; the roof was golden;
The doors were gates, most wonderfully carved;
The floor that used to be of earth was marble.
Jupiter, calm and grave, was speaking to them:
'You are good people, worthy of each other,
Good man, good wife – ask us for any favor,
And you shall have it.' And they hesitated,
Asked, 'Could we talk it over, just a little?'
And talked together, apart, and then Philemon

Spoke for them both: 'What we would like to be
Is to be priests of yours, and guard the temple,
And since we have spent our happy years together,
May one hour take us both away; let neither
Outlive the other, that I may never see
The burial of my wife, nor she perform
That office for me.' And the prayer was granted.
As long as life was given, they watched the temple,
And one day, as they stood before the portals,
Both very old, talking the old days over,
Each saw the other put forth leaves, Philemon
Watched Baucis changing, Baucis watched Philemon,
And as the foliage spread, they still had time
To say 'Farewell, my dear!' and the bark closed over
Sealing their mouths. And even to this day
The peasants in that district show the stranger
The two trees close together, and the union
Of oak and linden in one. The ones who told me
The story, sober ancients, were no liars,
Why should they be? And my own eyes have seen
The garlands people bring there; I brought new ones,
Myself, and said a verse: *The gods look after
Good people still, and cherishers are cherished.*

From LOVE

Used to each other to the point that we
no longer look to one another's gaze
to see what that could tell us; mirrorlike
it gives us back what we already are.
At least the baby's clear that we are two,
not of a kind. Biology doesn't tell him,
only the greener parent principle.
You go to him, he calls for Mama; me
he asks for Daddy. Even if for us
the grass has gone invisible with use
he sees it. So we keep each other green . . .

Love as the secret doubling of bodies
under the covers until the crisis birth
yanks them apart — then the long cutting of
the tail by inches. *By inchmeal a disease!*
shrieked Caliban, cursing the only parent
and teacher he had known. Love as, also,
two bodies only superficially one.
It took me years to learn to sleep with you —
real sleep, not euphemism, sinking back
on one another's silence. The centripetal/
centrifugal juggle of two matched affections . . .

I mother you you father me vice versa:
take the exhausted person off, discard
the mom and dadness of who's child, whose child
means less than the warm back we each of us
lie against, the body where we anchor
ourself, the imprint deep as blood. Perpetual
stoas, arcades, and alleys
loom and dwindle, mark our mutual
distance, proceeding down the avenue
clutching a clue, love's puzzle
not yet, not ever done.

RACHEL HADAS

SHE REVISITS ALONE THE
CHURCH OF HER MARRIAGE

I have come to the church and chancel,
     Where all's the same!
– Brighter and larger in my dreams
Truly it shaped than now, meseems,
     Is its substantial frame.
But, anyhow, I made my vow,
     Whether for praise or blame,
Here in this church and chancel
     Where all's the same.

Where touched the check-floored chancel
     My knees and his?
The step looks shyly at the sun,
And says, ' 'Twas here the thing was done,
     For bale or else for bliss!'
Of all those there I least was ware
     Would it be that or this
When touched the check-floored chancel
     My knees and his!

Here in this fateful chancel
       Where all's the same,
I thought the culminant crest of life
Was reached when I went forth the wife
       I was not when I came.
Each commonplace one of my race,
       Some say, has such an aim —
To go from a fateful chancel
       As not the same.

Here, through this hoary chancel
       Where all's the same,
A thrill, a gaiety even, ranged
That morning when it seemed I changed
       My nature with my name.
Though now not fair, though gray my hair,
       He loved me, past proclaim,
Here in this hoary chancel,
       Where all's the same.

THE PROGRESS OF MARRIAGE

Ætatis suæ fifty-two,
A rich Divine began to woo
A handsome, young, imperious girl,
Nearly related to an Earl.
Her parents and her friends consent,
The couple to the temple went:
They first invite the Cyprian Queen;
'Twas answer'd, she would not be seen:
The Graces next, and all the Muses
Were bid in form, but sent excuses.
Juno attended at the porch,
With farthing candle for a torch,
While Mistress Iris held her train,
The faded bow distilling rain.
Then Hebe came, and took her place,
But shew'd no more than half her face.

Whate'er those dire forebodings meant,
In mirth the wedding-day was spent;
The wedding-day, you take me right,
I promise nothing for the night.
The bridegroom drest, to make a figure
Assumes an artificial vigour;
A flourisht night-cap on, to grace
His ruddy, wrinkled, smiling face;

Like the faint red upon a pippin,
Half wither'd by a winter's keeping.

And, thus set out, this happy pair,
The Swain is rich, the Nymph is fair;
But, what I gladly would forget,
The Swain is old, the Nymph coquette.
Both from the goal together start;
Scarce run a step before they part;
No common ligament that binds
The various textures of their minds;
Their thoughts, and actions, hopes and fears,
Less corresponding than their years.
Her spouse desires his coffee soon,
She rises to her tea at noon.
While he goes out to cheapen books,
She at the lass consults her looks;
While Betty's buzzing in her ear,
Lord, what a dress these parsons wear!
So odd a choice how could she make?
Wisht him a Col'nel for her sake.
Then, on her fingers ends, she counts,
Exact, to what his age amounts.
The Dean, she heard her uncle say,
Is sixty, if he be a day;
His ruddy cheeks are no disguise;
You see the crows feet round his eyes.

At one she rambles to the shops,
To cheapen tea, and talk with fops;
Or calls a council of her maids,
And tradesmen, to compare brocades.
Her weighty morning bus'ness o'er,
Sits down to dinner just at four;
Minds nothing that is done or said,
Her ev'ning work so fills her head,
The Dean, who us'd to dine at one,
Is maukish, and his stomach gone;
In thread-bare gown, would scarce a louse hold,
Looks like the chaplain of his houshold,
Beholds her from the chaplain's place
In French brocades and Flanders lace;
He wonders what employs her brain,
But never asks, or asks in vain;
His mind is full of other cares,
And, in the sneaking parson's airs,
Computes, that half a parish dues
Will hardly find his wife in shoes.

Can'st thou imagine, dull Divine,
'Twill gain her love to make her fine?
Hath she no other wants beside?
You raise desire as well as pride,
Enticing coxcombs to adore,
And teach her to despise thee more.

If in her coach she'll condescend
To place him at the hinder end
Her hoop is hoist above his nose,
His odious gown would soil her cloaths,
And drops him at the church, to pray,
While she drives on to see the Play.
He, like an orderly divine,
Comes home a quarter after nine,
And meets her hasting to the ball:
Her chairmen push him from the wall.
He enters in, and walks up stairs,
And calls the family to pray'rs;
Then goes alone to take his rest
In bed, where he can spare her best.
At five the footmen make a din,
Her Ladyship is just come in,
The masquerade began at two,
She stole away with much ado;
And shall be chid this afternoon
For leaving company so soon:
She'll say, and she may truly say't,
She can't abide to stay out late.

But now, though scarce a twelvemonth
    marry'd,
Poor Lady Jane has thrice miscarry'd:
The cause, alas, is quickly guest,

The town has whisper'd round the jest.
Think on some remedy in time,
You find his Rev'rence past his prime,
Already dwindled to a lath;
No other way but try the Bath.

For Venus rising from the ocean,
Infus'd a strong prolifick potion,
That mixt with Achelaus' spring,
The *horned* flood, as poets sing,
Who, with an English beauty smitten,
Ran underground from Greece to Britain;
The genial virtue with him brought,
And gave the Nymph a plenteous draught;
Then fled, and left his horn behind
For husbands past their youth to find:
The Nymph, who still with passion burn'd,
Was to a boiling fountain turn'd,
Where childless wives croud ev'ry morn
To drink in Achelaus' horn.
And here the father often gains
That title by another's pains.

Hither, though much against the grain,
The Dean has carry'd Lady Jane.
He, for a while, would not consent,
But vow'd his money all was spent:

His money spent! a clownish reason!
And must my Lady slip her season?
The Doctor with a double fee,
Was brib'd to make the Dean agree.

Here all diversions of the place
Are proper in my Lady's case:
With which she patiently complies,
Merely because her friends advise;
His money and her time employs
In Musick, raffling-rooms and toys;
Or, in the *Cross-bath*, seeks an heir,
Since others oft have found one there:
Where, if the Dean by chance appears,
It shames his cassock and his years.
He keeps his distance in the gallery
'Till banish'd by some coxcomb's raillery;
For, 'twould his character expose
To bathe among the belles and beaux.

So have I seen, within a pen,
Young ducklings foster'd by a hen;
But, when let out, they run and muddle,
As instinct leads them, in a puddle:
The sober hen, not born to swim,
With mournful note clucks round the brim.

The Dean, with all his best endeavour,
Gets not an heir, but gets a fever,
A victim to the last essays
Of vigor in declining days,
He dies, and leaves his mourning mate
(What could he less?) his whole estate.

The widow goes through all her forms:
New Lovers now will come in swarms.
Oh, may I see her soon dispensing
Her favours to some broken ensign!
Him let her marry, for his face,
And only coat of tarnisht lace;
To turn her naked out of doors,
And spend her jointure on his whores:
But, for a parting present, leave her
A rooted pox to last for ever.

AT TEA

The kettle descants in a cosy drone,
And the young wife looks in her husband's face,
And then at her guest's, and shows in her own
Her sense that she fills an envied place;
And the visiting lady is all abloom,
And says there was never so sweet a room.

And the happy young housewife does not know
That the woman beside her was first his choice,
Till the fates ordained it could not be so . . .
Betraying nothing in look or voice
The guest sits smiling and sips her tea,
And he throws her a stray glance yearningly.

'TO SPEAK OF WOE THAT IS
IN MARRIAGE'

It is the future generation that presses into being by means of these exuberant feelings and supersensible soap bubbles of ours.

SCHOPENHAUER

'The hot night makes us keep our bedroom windows
      open.
Our magnolia blossoms. Life begins to happen.
My hopped up husband drops his home disputes,
and hits the streets to cruise for prostitutes,
free-lancing out along the razor's edge.
This screwball might kill his wife, then take the pledge.
Oh the monotonous meanness of his lust . . .
It's the injustice . . . he is so unjust –
whiskey-blind, swaggering home at five.
My only thought is how to keep alive.
What makes him tick? Each night now I tie
ten dollars and his car key to my thigh . . .
Gored by the climacteric of his want,
he stalls above me like an elephant.'

BEFORE THE BIRTH OF ONE HER CHILDREN

All things within this fading world hath end,
Adversity doth still our joyes attend;
No tyes so strong, no friends so dear and sweet,
But with deaths parting blow is sure to meet.
The sentence past is most irrevocable,
A common thing, yet oh inevitable;
How soon, my Dear, death may my steps attend,
How soon't may be thy Lot to lose thy friend,
We both are ignorant, yet love bids me
These farewell lines to recommend to thee,
That when that knot's unty'd that made us one,
I may seem thine, who in effect am none.
And if I see not half my dayes that's due,
What nature would, God grant to yours and you;
The many faults that well you know I have,
Let be interr'd in my oblivious grave;
If any worth or virtue were in me,
Let that live freshly in thy memory
And when thou feel'st no grief, as I no harms,
Yet love thy dead, who long lay in thine arms:
And when thy loss shall be repaid with gains
Look to my little babes my dear remains.
And if thou love thy self, or loved'st me
These O protect from step Dames injury.

And if chance to thine eyes shall bring this verse,
With some sad sighs honour my absent Herse;
And kiss this paper for thy loves dear sake,
Who with salt tears this last Farewel did take.

DISCOURSE

With thee conversing, I forget all time,
All seasons, and their change; all please alike.
Sweet is the breath of Morn, her rising sweet,
With charm of earliest birds; pleasant the Sun,
When first on this delightful land he spreads
His orient beams, on herb, tree, fruit, and flower,
Glist'ring with dew; fragrant the fertile Earth
After soft showers; and sweet the coming-on
Of grateful Evening mild; then silent Night,
With this her solemn bird, and this fair Moon,
And these the gems of Heaven, her starry train:
But neither breath of Morn, when she ascends
With charm of earliest birds; nor rising Sun
On this delightful land; nor herb, fruit, flower,
Glist'ring with dew; nor fragrance after showers:
Nor grateful Evening mild; nor silent Night,
With this her solemn bird; nor walk by moon,
Or glittering starling, without thee is sweet.

THE TELEPHONE

'When I was just as far as I could walk
From here today,
There was an hour
All still
When leaning with my head against a flower
I heard you talk.
Don't say I didn't, for I heard you say –
You spoke from that flower on the window sill –
Do you remember what it was you said?'

'First tell me what it was you thought you heard.'

'Having found the flower and driven a bee away,
I leaned my head,
And holding by the stalk,
I listened and I thought I caught the word –
What was it? Did you call me by my name?
Or did you say –
Someone said "Come" – I heard it as I bowed.'

'I may have thought as much, but not aloud.'

'Well, so I came.'

UPON JOLLY AND JILLY

Jolly and Jilly bite and scratch all day,
But yet get children (as the neighbors say.)
The reason is, though all the day they fight,
They cling and close, some minutes of the night.

ROBERT HERRICK

MODERN MARRIAGE

By this he knew she wept with waking eyes:
That, at his hand's light quiver by her head,
The strange low sobs that shook their common bed,
Were called into her with a sharp surprise,
And strangled mute, like little gaping snakes,
Dreadfully venomous to him. She lay
Stone-still, and the long darkness flowed away
With muffled pulses. Then, as midnight makes
Her giant heart of Memory and Tears
Drink the pale drug of silence, and so beat
Sleep's heavy measure, they from head to feet
Were moveless, looking through their dead black
      years,
By vain regret scrawled over the blank wall.
Like sculptured effigies they might be seen
Upon their marriage-tomb, the sword between;
Each wishing for the sword that severs all.

NUPTIAL SLEEP

At length their long kiss severed, with sweet smart:
   And as the last slow sudden drops are shed
   From sparkling eaves when all the storm has fled,
So singly flagged the pulses of each heart.
Their bosoms sundered, with the opening start
   Of married flowers to either side outspread
   From the knit stem; yet still their mouths, burnt red,
Fawned on each other where they lay apart.

Sleep sank them lower than the tide of dreams,
   And their dreams watched them sink, and slid away.
Slowly their souls swam up again, through gleams
   Of watered light and dull drowned waifs of day;
Till from some wonder of new woods and streams
   He woke, and wondered more: for there she lay.

WITCH-WIFE

She is neither pink nor pale,
    And she never will be all mine;
She learned her hands in a fairy-tale,
    And her mouth on a valentine.

She has more hair than she needs;
    In the sun 'tis a woe to me!
And her voice is a string of coloured beads,
    Or steps leading into the sea.

She loves me all that she can,
    And her ways to my ways resign;
But she was not made for any man,
    And she never will be all mine.

THE HILL WIFE

I. LONELINESS
Her Word
One ought not to have to care
    So much as you and I
Care when the birds come round the house
    To seem to say good-by;

Or care so much when they come back
    With whatever it is they sing;
The truth being we are as much
    Too glad for the one thing

As we are too sad for the other here –
    With birds that fill their breasts
But with each other and themselves
    And their built or driven nests.

II. HOUSE FEAR
Always – I tell you this they learned –
Always at night when they returned
To the lonely house from far away,
To lamps unlighted and fire gone gray,
They learned to rattle the lock and key
To give whatever might chance to be,
Warning and time to be off in flight:

And preferring the out- to the indoor night,
They learned to leave the house door wide
Until they had lit the lamp inside.

III. THE SMILE
Her Word
I didn't like the way he went away.
That smile! It never came of being gay.
Still he smiled – did you see him? – I was sure!
Perhaps because we gave him only bread
And the wretch knew from that that we were poor.
Perhaps because he let us give instead
Of seizing from us as he might have seized.
Perhaps he mocked at us for being wed,
Or being very young (and he was pleased
To have a vision of us old and dead).
I wonder how far down the road he's got.
He's watching from the woods as like as not.

IV. THE OFT-REPEATED DREAM
She had no saying dark enough
    For the dark pine that kept
Forever trying the window latch
    Of the room where they slept.

The tireless but ineffectual hands
    That with every futile pass

Made the great tree seem as a little bird
    Before the mystery of glass!

It never had been inside the room,
    And only one of the two
Was afraid in an oft-repeated dream
    Of what the tree might do.

V. THE IMPULSE

It was too lonely for her there,
    And too wild,
And since there were but two of them,
    And no child,

And work was little in the house,
    She was free,
And followed where he furrowed field,
    Or felled tree.

She rested on a log and tossed
    The fresh chips,
With a song only to herself
    On her lips.

And once she went to break a bough
    Of black alder.
She strayed so far she scarcely heard
    When he called her –

And didn't answer – didn't speak –
    Or return.
She stood, and then she ran and hid
    In the fern.

He never found her, though he looked
    Everywhere,
And he asked at her mother's house
    Was she there.

Sudden and swift and light as that
    The ties gave,
And he learned of finalities
    Besides the grave.

THE HOUSEHOLDER

Savage I was sitting in my house, late, lone:
    Dreary, weary with the long day's work:
Head of me, heart of me, stupid as a stone;
    Tongue-tied now, blaspheming like a Turk;
When, in a moment, just a knock, call, cry,
    Half a pang and all a rapture, there again were we! –
'What, and is it really you again?' quoth I:
    'I again, what else did you expect?' quoth She.

'Never mind, hie away from this old house –
    Every crumbling brick embrowned with sin and
        shame!
Quick, in its corner ere certain shapes arouse!
    Let them – every devil of the night – lay claim,
Make and mend, or rap and rend, for me! Goodbye!
    God be their guard from all disturbance of their
        glee,
Till, crash, comes down the carcass in a heap!' quoth I:
    'Nay, but there's a decency required!' quoth She.

'Ah, but if you knew how time has dragged, days,
      nights!
   All the neighbour-talk with man and maid – such
      men!
All the fuss and trouble of street-sounds, window-
      sights:
   All the worry of flapping door and echoing roof;
      and then,
All the fancies . . . Who were they had leave, dared try
   Darker arts that almost struck despair in me?
If you knew but how I dwelt down here!' quoth I:
   'And was I so better off up there?' quoth She.

'Help and get it over! *Re-united to his wife*
   (How draw up the paper lets the parish-people
      know?)
Lies M., or N., departed from this life,
   Day the this or that, month and year the so and so.
What i' the way of final flourish? Prose, verse? Try!
   Affliction sore long time he bore, or what is it to be?
Till God did please to grant him ease. Do end!' quoth I:
   'I end with – Love is all and Death is nought!'
      quoth She.

TITHONUS

The woods decay, the woods decay and fall,
The vapours weep their burthen to the ground,
Man comes and tills the field and lies beneath,
And after many a summer dies the swan.
Me only cruel immortality
Consumes: I wither slowly in thine arms,
Here at the quiet limit of the world,
A white-hair'd shadow roaming like a dream
The ever-silent spaces of the East,
Far-folded mists, and gleaming halls of morn.

Alas! for this gray shadow, once a man –
So glorious in his beauty and thy choice,
Who madest him thy chosen, that he seem'd
To his great heart none other than a God!
I ask'd thee, 'Give me immortality.'
Then didst thou grant mine asking with a smile,
Like wealthy men who care not how they give.
But thy strong Hours indignant work'd their wills,
And beat me down and marr'd and wasted me,
And tho' they could not end me, left me maim'd
To dwell in presence of immortal youth,
Immortal age beside immortal youth,
And all I was, in ashes. Can thy love,
Thy beauty, make amends, tho' even now,

Close over us, the silver star, thy guide,
Shines in those tremulous eyes that fill with tears
To hear me? Let me go: take back thy gift:
Why should a man desire in any way
To vary from the kindly race of men,
Or pass beyond the goal of ordinance
Where all should pause, as is most meet for all?

A soft air fans the cloud apart; there comes
A glimpse of that dark world where I was born.
Once more the old mysterious glimmer steals
From thy pure brows, and from thy shoulders pure,
And bosom beating with a heart renew'd.
Thy cheek begins to redden thro' the gloom,
Thy sweet eyes brighten slowly close to mine,
Ere yet they blind the stars, and the wild team
Which love thee, yearning for thy yoke, arise,
And shake the darkness from their loosen'd manes,
And beat the twilight into flakes of fire.

Lo! ever thus thou growest beautiful
In silence, then before thine answer given
Departest, and thy tears are on my cheek.

Why wilt thou ever scare me with thy tears,
And make me tremble lest a saying learnt,
In days far-off, on that dark earth, be true?
'The Gods themselves cannot recall their gifts.'

Ay me! ay me! with what another heart
In days far-off, and with what other eyes
I used to watch – if I be he that watch'd –
The lucid outline forming round thee; saw
The dim curls kindle into sunny rings;
Changed with thy mystic change, and felt my blood
Glow with the glow that slowly crimson'd all
Thy presence and thy portals, while I lay,
Mouth, forehead, eyelids, growing dewy-warm
With kisses balmier than half-opening buds
Of April, and could hear the lips that kiss'd
Whispering I knew not what of wild and sweet,
Like that strange song I heard Apollo sing,
While Ilion like a mist rose into towers.

Yet hold me not for ever in thine East:
How can my nature longer mix with thine?
Coldly thy rosy shadows bathe me, cold
Are all thy lights, and cold my wrinkled feet
Upon thy glimmering thresholds, when the steam
Floats up from those dim fields about the homes
Of happy men that have the power to die,
And grassy barrows of the happier dead.
Release me, and restore me to the ground;
Thou seëst all things, thou wilt see my grave:
Thou wilt renew thy beauty morn by morn;
I earth in earth forget these empty courts,
And thee returning on thy silver wheels.

ALFRED, LORD TENNYSON   123

ANNIVERSARIES

All Kings, and all their favorites,
All glory of honors, beauties, wits,
The Sun it selfe, which makes times, as they pass,
Is elder by a year, now, than it was
When thou and I first one another saw:
All other things, to their destruction draw,
    Only our love hath no decay;
This, no to morrow hath, nor yesterday,
Running it never runs from us away,
But truly keeps his first, last, everlasting day.

JOHN DONNE

SILVER WEDDING

The Silver Wedding! on some pensive ear
   From towers remote as sound the silvery bells,
To-day from one far unforgotten year
   A silvery faint memorial music swells.

And silver-pale the dim memorial light
   Of musing age on youthful joys is shed,
The golden joys of fancy's dawning bright,
   The golden bliss of, Woo'd, and won, and wed.

Ah, golden then, but silver now! In sooth,
   The years that pale the cheek, that dim the eyes,
And silver o'er the golden hairs of youth,
   Less prized can make its only priceless prize.

Not so; the voice this silver name that gave
   To this, the ripe and unenfeebled date,
For steps together tottering to the grave,
   Hath bid the perfect golden title wait.

Rather, if silver this, if that be gold,
   From good to better changed on age's track,
Must it as baser metal be enrolled,
   That day of days, a quarter-century back.

Yet ah, its hopes, its joys were golden too,
  But golden of the fairy gold of dreams:
To feel is but to dream; until we do,
  There's nought that is, and all we see but seems.

What was or seemed it needed cares and tears,
  And deeds together done, and trials past,
And all the subtlest alchemy of years,
  To change to genuine substance here at last.

Your fairy gold is silver sure to-day;
  Your ore by crosses many, many a loss,
As in refiners' fires, hath purged away
  What erst it had of earthy human dross.

Come years as many yet, and as they go,
  In human life's great crucible shall they
Transmute, so potent are the spells they know,
  Into pure gold the silver of to-day.

Strange metallurge is human life! 'Tis true!
  And Use and Wont in many a gorgeous case
Full specious fair for casual outward view
  Electrotype the sordid and the base.

Nor lack who praise, avowed, the spurious ware,
    Who bid young hearts the one true love forego,
Conceit to feed, or fancy light as air,
    Or greed of pelf and precedence and show.

True, false, as one to casual eyes appear,
    To read men truly men may hardly learn;
Yet doubt it not that wariest glance would here
    Faith, Hope and Love, the true Tower-stamp discern.

Come years again! as many yet! and purge
    Less precious earthier elements away,
And gently changed at life's extremest verge,
    Bring bright in gold your perfect fiftieth day!

That sight may children see and parents show!
    If not – yet earthly chains of metal true,
By love and duty wrought and fixed below,
    Elsewhere will shine, transformed, celestial-new;

Will shine of gold, whose essence, heavenly bright,
    No doubt-damps tarnish, worldly passions fray;
Gold into gold there mirrored, light in light,
    Shall gleam in glories of a deathless day.

ARTHUR HUGH CLOUGH   129

A SECOND RING

'Thee, Mary, with this ring I wed,'
So, fourteen years ago, I said.
Behold another ring! 'For what?'
To wed thee o'er again – why not?

With that first ring I married youth,
Grace, beauty, innocence, and truth;
Taste long admired, sense long revered,
And all my Molly then appeared.

If she, by merit since disclosed,
Prove twice the woman I supposed,
I plead that double merit now,
To justify a double vow.

Here then, to-day, – with faith as sure,
With ardour as intense and pure,
As when amidst the rites divine
I took thy troth, and plighted mine, –
To thee, sweet girl, my second ring,
A token, and a pledge, I bring;
With this I wed, till death us part,
Thy riper virtues to my heart;
Those virtues which, before untried,
The wife has added to the bride –

Those virtues, whose progressive claim,
Endearing wedlock's very name,
My soul enjoys, my song approves,
For conscience' sake as well as love's.

For why? – They show me every hour
Honour's high thought, affection's power,
Discretion's deed, sound judgment's sentence,
And teach me all things – but repentance.

JEÄNE

We now mid hope vor better cheer,
My smilèn wife o' twice vive year.
Let others frown, if thou bist near
     Wi' hope upon thy brow, Jeäne;
Vor I vu'st lov'd thee when thy light
Young sheäpe vu'st grew to woman's height;
I loved thee near, an' out o' zight,
     An' I do love thee now, Jeäne.

An' we've a-trod the sheenèn bleäde
Ov eegrass in the summer sheäde,
An' when the leäves begun to feäde
     Wi' zummer in the weäne, Jeäne;
And we've a-wander'd drough the groun'
O' swayèn wheat a-turnèn brown,
An' we've a-stroll'd together roun'
     The brook an' drough the leäne, Jeäne.

An' nwone but I can ever tell
Ov all thy tears that have a-vell
When trials meäde thy bosom zwell,
     An' nwone but thou o' mine, Jeäne;
An' now my heart, that heaved wi' pride
Back then to have thee at my zide,
Do love thee mwore as years do slide,
     An' leäve them times behind, Jeäne.

ON AN ANNIVERSARY

Thirty years and more go by
In the blinking of an eye,
    And you are still the same
As when first you took my name.

Much the same blush now as then
Glimmers through the peach-pale skin.
    Time (but as with a glove)
Lightly touches you, my love.

Stand with me a minute still
While night climbs our little hill.
    Below, the lights of cars
Move, and overhead the stars.

The estranging years that come,
Come and go, and we are home.
    Time joins us as a friend,
And the evening has no end.

ON A WEDDING ANNIVERSARY

The sky is torn across
This ragged anniversary of two
Who moved for three years in tune
Down the long walks of their vows.

Now their love lies a loss
And Love and his patients roar on a chain;
From every true or crater
Carrying cloud, Death strikes their house.

Too late in the wrong rain
They come together whom their love parted:
The windows pour into their heart
And the doors burn in their brain.

THE MARRIAGE

Incarnate for our marriage you appeared,
Flesh living in the spirit and endeared
By minor graces and slow sensual change.
Through every nerve we made our spirits range.
We fed our minds on every mortal thing:
The lacy fronds of carrots in the spring,
Their flesh sweet on the tongue, the salty wine
From bitter grapes, which gathered through the vine
The mineral drouth of autumn concentrate,
Wild spring in dream escaping, the debate
Of flesh and spirit on those vernal nights,
Its resolution in naive delights,
The young kids bleating softly in the rain –
All this to pass, not to return again.
And when I found your flesh did not resist,
It was the living spirit that I kissed,
It was the spirit's change in which I lay:
Thus, mind in mind we waited for the day.
When flesh shall fall away, and, falling, stand
Wrinkling with shadow over face and hand,
Still I shall meet you on the verge of dust
And know you as a faithful vestige must.
And, in commemoration of our lust,
May our heirs seal us in a single urn,
A single spirit never to return.

YVOR WINTERS   135

THE COMMEMORATION

I wish I could proclaim
My faith enshrined in you
And spread among a few
Our high but hidden fame,
That we new life have spun
Past all that's thought and done,
And someone or no one
Might tell both did the same.

Material things will pass
And we have seen the flower
And the slow falling tower
Lie gently in the grass,
But meantime we have stored
Riches past bed and board
And nursed another hoard
Than callow lad and lass.

Invisible virtue now
Expands upon the air
Although no fruit appear
Nor weight bend down the bough,
And harvests truly grown
For someone or no one
Are stored and safely won
In hollow heart and brow.

How can one thing remain
Except the invisible,
The echo of a bell
Long rusted in the rain?
This strand we weave into
Our monologue of two,
And time cannot undo
That strong and subtle chain.

TO MY WIFE

And does the heart grow old? You know
In the indiscriminate green
Of summer or in earliest snow
A landscape is another scene,

Inchoate and anonymous,
And every rock and bush and drift
As our affections alter us
Will alter with the season's shift.

So love by love we come at last,
As through the exclusions of a rhyme,
Or the exactions of a past,
To the simplicity of time,

The antiquity of grace, where yet
We live in terror and delight
With love as quiet as regret
And love like anger in the night.

JOHN ANDERSON MY JO

John Anderson my jo, John,
　　When we were first acquent;
Your locks were like the raven,
　　Your bony brow was brent;
But now your brow is beld, John,
　　Your locks are like the snaw;
But blessings on your frosty pow,
　　John Anderson my Jo.

John Anderson my jo, John,
　　We clamb the hill the gither;
And mony a canty day, John,
　　We've had wi' ane anither:
Now we maun totter down, John,
　　And hand in hand we'll go;
And sleep the gither at the foot,
　　John Anderson my jo.

ROBERT BURNS

AN EPITAPH UPON HUSBAND
AND WIFE WHO DIED AND
WERE BURIED TOGETHER

To these whom death again did wed
This grave's the second marriage-bed.
For though the hand of Fate could force
'Twixt soul and body a divorce,
It could not sever man and wife,
Because they both lived but one life.
Peace, good reader, do not weep;
Peace, the lovers are asleep.
They, sweet turtles, folded lie
In the last knot that love could tie.
Let them sleep, let them sleep on,
Till the stormy night be gone,
And the eternal morrow dawn;
Then the curtains will be drawn,
And they wake into a light
Whose day shall never die in night.

ADULTERIES

Barking at thieves, silent when lovers came,
I pleased at once my master and my dame.

JOACHIM DU BELLAY, *On the Tomb of a Dog*
TRANSLATED BY JOHN HOLLANDER

A FOOLISH MARRIAGE VOW

1

Why should a foolish marriage vow
   Which long ago was made,
Oblige us to each other now
   When passion is decayed?
We loved, and we loved, as long as we could,
   Till our love was loved out in us both.
But our marriage is dead, when the pleasure is fled:
   'Twas pleasure first made it an oath.

2

If I have pleasures for a friend,
   And farther love in store,
What wrong has he whose joys did end,
   And who could give no more?
'Tis a madness that he should be jealous of me,
   Or that I should bar him of another;
For all we can gain is to give ourselves pain,
   When neither can hinder the other.

JOHN DRYDEN

MENELAUS AND HELEN

I

Hot through Troy's ruin Menelaus broke
   To Priam's palace, sword in hand, to sate
   On that adulterous whore a ten years' hate
And a king's honour. Through red death, and smoke,
And cries, and then by quieter ways he strode,
   Till the still innermost chamber fronted him.
   He swung his sword, and crashed into the dim
Luxurious bower, flaming like a god.

High sat white Helen, lonely and serene.
   He had not remembered that she was so fair,
And that her neck curved down in such a way;
And he felt tired. He flung the sword away,
   And kissed her feet, and knelt before her there,
The perfect Knight before the perfect Queen.

So far the poet. How should he behold
    That journey home, the long connubial years?
    He does not tell you how white Helen bears
Child on legitimate child, becomes a scold,
Haggard with virtue. Menelaus bold
    Waxed garrulous, and sacked a hundred Troys
    'Twixt noon and supper. And her golden voice
Got shrill as he grew deafer. And both were old.

Often he wonders why on earth he went
    Troyward, or why poor Paris ever came.
Oft she weeps, gummy-eyed and impotent;
    Her dry shanks twist at Paris' mumbled name.
So Menelaus nagged; and Helen cried;
And Paris slept on by Scamander side.

RUPERT BROOKE   145

THE WRAGGLE TAGGLE GIPSIES

There were three gipsies a-come to my door,
And downstairs ran this a-lady, O!
One sang high, and another sang low,
And the other sang bonny, bonny Biscay, O!

Then she pulled off her silk-finished gown
And put on hose of leather, O!
The ragged, ragged rags about our door –
She's gone with the wraggle taggle gipsies, O!

It was late last night, when my lord came home,
Enquiring for his a-lady, O!
The servants said, on every hand:
She's gone with the wraggle taggle gipsies, O!

O saddle to me my milk-white steed.
Go and fetch me my pony, O!
That I may ride and seek my bride,
Who is gone with the wraggle taggle gipsies, O!

O he rode high and he rode low,
He rode through woods and copses too,
Until he came to an open field,
And there he espied his a-lady, O!

What makes you leave your house and land?
What makes you leave your money, O?
What makes you leave your new-wedded lord;
To go with the wraggle taggle gipsies, O?

What care I for my house and my land?
What care I for my money, O?
What care I for my new-wedded lord?
I'm off with the wraggle taggle gipsies, O!

Last night you slept on a goose-feather bed,
With the sheet turned down so bravely, O!
And to-night you'll sleep in a cold open field,
Along with the wraggle taggle gipsies, O!

What care I for a goose-feather bed,
With the sheet turned down so bravely, O?
For to-night I shall sleep in a cold open field,
Along with the wraggle taggle gipsies, O!

ANONYMOUS

MY MOTHER MADE
ME MARRY

My mother made me marry,
When I was pretty and little,
A rogue, a boy,
Whom I didn't love at all.
When it struck midnight
Out went the rogue,
Cloak on shoulder
And his sword slung on.
I followed his footsteps
To see where he would go,
And I saw him enter
His lady-love's house.
I went close to listen
To hear what he would say
And I heard him tell her:
– For you, my little dove,
I intend to purchase
Petticoats and shawls,
And I'll give that other woman
A stick and bad times. –
I went back home
In sorrow and dismay.
I sat down to eat
But eat I could not,

I sat down to sew
But sew I could not,
I got down to pray
But pray I could not.
I went to the balcony
To see if he was coming.
I heard his footsteps
Coming up the street.
He came to the door
And he called out and said:
– Open to me, open to me,
Open the door, love,
For I've come home weary
From making us a living. –
– You've come home, liar,
From your lady-love,
I distinctly heard you tell her:
– For you, my little dove,
I intend to purchase
Petticoats and shawls,
And I'll give that other woman
A stick and bad times.

ANONYMOUS, SPANISH

TRANSLATED BY W. S. MERWIN

THE FLOWER-GIRL

I am slim as a betel leaf
And lovely as a flower,
My husband goes to Madhuban
And flirts with the flower-girl.
Join me, my friends,
Come in a crowd to Madhuban
And look at my husband's temple.
To one wood they go
To another they go
In the third wood, O little one,
They see the husband's temple
Where he flirts with the flower-girl.
'O flower-girl, with your wiles
How did you enchant the king
And what delight do you give him?'
'O lovely lady,
I spread betel leaves and scatter blossoms
I fan him the whole night
And I bewitch him with my eyes.'

150   ANONYMOUS, INDIAN
        TRANSLATED BY W. G. ARCHER

THE ART OF DECEIVING A HUSBAND

I was about to omit the art of deceiving a husband,
    Fooling a vigilant guard, crafty though either might be.
Let the bride honor, obey, pay proper respect to her
       husband,
    That is only correct; decency says so, and law.
But why should you, set free, and not too long ago, either,
    By the decree of the court, have to be kept like a bride?
Listen to me, and learn; though your watchers are there
       by the hundred,
    If you will take my advice, you can get rid of them all.
How can they interfere or stop you from writing a letter?
    What is a bathroom for? Tell them you have to go
       there.
Haven't you any close friend who knows how to carry
       a tablet
    Under her arm, or perhaps tucked in the fold
       of a gown?
Isn't she able to hide a note in the top of her stocking,
    Or, if that's apt to be found, in the instep of a shoe?
Is her guardian on to such tricks? – let her offer herself
       as a tablet,
    Carry, in code, on her back, letters in lipstick of red.
For your invisible ink, use milk: it will show when you
       heat it;
    Write with a stem of wet flax – no one will ever suspect.

Danae's father supposed he was careful in guarding
    his daughter;
  He was a grandfather soon, proving his vigilance vain.
What can a guardian do, with theaters all through the city?
  What can a guardian do when a girl goes to the track?
What can he do when she kneels to offer her homage
    to Isis?
  That is a place where no man ever has freedom to go.
There are more temples than one from which male eyes
    are forbidden,
  Where the Good Goddess allows only her servants
    to come.
What can a guardian do but sit and look at her clothing
  When a girl goes to the baths, finding her games and
    her fun?
What is the use? She must go to take care of a friend,
    in a sickroom;
  Then her friend's perfectly well, leaving her half
    of the bed.
What can be done when the town is full of experienced
    locksmiths,
  When it's not only the door letting you enter at will?
Even the cheapest wine from Spain will befuddle a
    guardian;
  Drugs are effective as well, working with opiate spell.
He can be put to sleep if you send your maid to seduce him,
  Keeping him by her side, joined in delightful delay.

152

Why do I waste so much time with all this instruction
       in detail?
   There is an easier way; it won't take much of a bribe.
Take my word for it, bribes can buy both men and
       immortals;
   Jupiter, even, is won if you bring gifts to his shrine.
Fools will brag about bribes, but what can be done with a
       wise man?
   Bribe him. He'll take the bribe; furthermore, he will
       keep still.
But remember one thing – you're paying for permanent
       service,
   Yours is a long-term lease; see that the bribe is enough.
I recall making complaints about friends who were not to
       be trusted:
   This, you can be very sure, happens not only with men.
Don't trust the other girls: they'll steal your man in a
       second,
   Hunters, that's what they are, having no conscience
       at all.
Also, beware of the friend who has a spare room for
       your lover.
   I know how that works out; I've been there many a time.
One final word of advice: don't let your maid be too pretty –
   Often a maid will do all you would like to, and more.

IN THE RESTAURANT

'But hear. If you stay, and the child be born,
It will pass as your husband's with the rest,
While, if we fly, the teeth of scorn
Will be gleaming at us from east to west;
And the child will come as a life despised;
I feel an elopement is ill-advised!'

'O you realize not what it is, my dear,
To a woman! Daily and hourly alarms
Lest the truth should out. How can I stay here
And nightly take him into my arms!
Come to the child no name or fame,
Let us go, and face it, and bear the shame.'

GUESTS FOR DINNER

At dinner, she is hostess, I am host.
Went the feast ever cheerfuller? She keeps
The Topic over intellectual deeps
In buoyancy afloat. They see no ghost.
With sparkling surface-eyes we ply the ball:
It is in truth a most contagious game:
HIDING THE SKELETON, shall be its name.
Such play as this, the devils might appal!
But here's the greater wonder; in that we
Enamoured of an acting nought can tire,
Each other, like true hypocrites, admire;
Warm-lighted looks, Love's ephemerioe,
Shoot gaily o'er the dishes and the wine.
We waken envy of our happy lot.
Fast, sweet, and golden, shows the marriage-knot.
Dear guests, you now have seen Love's corpse-light
     shine.

HARP SONG OF THE DANE WOMEN
'THE KNIGHTS OF THE JOYOUS VENTURE'
— PUCK OF POOK'S HILL

What is a woman that you forsake her,
And the hearth-fire and the home-acre,
To go with the old grey Widow-maker?

She has no house to lay a guest in –
But one chill bed for all to rest in,
That the pale suns and the stray bergs nest in.

She has no strong white arms to fold you,
But the ten-times-fingering weed to hold you –
Out on the rocks where the tide has rolled you.

Yet, when the signs of summer thicken,
And the ice breaks, and the birch-buds quicken,
Yearly you turn from our side, and sicken –

Sicken again for the shouts and the slaughters.
You steal away to the lapping waters,
And look at your ship in her winter-quarters.

You forget our mirth, and talk at the tables,
The kine in the shed and the horse in the stables –
To pitch her sides and go over her cables.

Then you drive out where the storm-clouds swallow,
And the sound of your oar-blades, falling hollow,
Is all we have left through the months to follow.

Ah, what is Woman that you forsake her,
And the hearth-fire and the home-acre,
To go with the old grey Widow-maker?

THE TRIANGLE

Madam would speak with me. So, now it comes:
The Deluge or else Fire! She's well; she thanks
My husbandship. Our chain on silence clanks.
Time leers between, above his twiddling thumbs.
Am I quite well? Most excellent in health!
The journals, too, I diligently peruse.
Vesuvius is expected to give news:
Niagara is no noisier. By stealth
Our eyes dart scrutinizing snakes. She's glad
I'm happy, says her quivering under-lip.
'And are not you?' 'How can I be?' 'Take ship!
For happiness is somewhere to be had.'
'Nowhere for me!' Her voice is barely heard.
I am not melted, and make no pretence.
With commonplace I freeze her, tongue and sense.
Niagara or Vesuvius is deferred.

It is no vulgar nature I have wived.
Secretive, sensitive, she takes a wound
Deep to her soul, as if the sense had swooned,
And not a thought of vengeance had survived.
No confidences has she: but relief
Must come to one whose suffering is acute.
O have a care of natures that are mute!
They punish you in acts: their steps are brief.

What is she doing? What does she demand
From Providence or me? She is not one
Long to endure this torpidly, and shun
The drugs that crowd about a woman's hand.
At Forfeits during snow we played, and I
Must kiss her. 'Well performed!' I said: then she:
' 'T is hardly worth the money, you agree?'
Save her? What for? To act this wedded lie!

My Lady unto Madam makes her bow.
The charm of women is, that even while
You're probed by them for tears, you yet may smile,
Nay, laugh outright, as I have done just now.
The interview was gracious: they anoint
(To me aside) each other with fine praise:
Discriminating compliments they raise,
That hit with wondrous aim on the weak point:
My Lady's nose of Nature might complain.
It is not fashioned aptly to express
Her character of large-browed steadfastness.
But Madam says: Thereof she may be vain!
Now, Madam's faulty feature is a glazed
And inaccessible eye, that has soft fires,
Wide gates, at love-time only. This admires
My Lady. At the two I stand amazed.

ADULTERY

We have all been in rooms
We cannot die in, and they are odd places, and sad.
Often Indians are standing eagle-armed on hills

In the sunrise   open wide to the Great Spirit
Or gliding in canoes   or cattle are browsing on the walls
Far away   gazing down with the eyes of our children

Not far away   or there are men driving
The last railspike, which has turned
Gold in their hands. Gigantic forepleasure lives

Among such scenes, and we are alone with it
At last. There is always some weeping
Between us   and someone is always checking

A wrist watch by the bed to see how much
Longer we have left. Nothing can come
Of this   nothing can come

Of us: of me with my grim techniques
Or you who have sealed your womb
With a ring of convulsive rubber:

Although we come together,
Nothing will come of us. But we would not give
It up, for death is beaten

By praying Indians   by distant cows   historical
Hammers   by hazardous meetings that bridge
A continent. One could never die here

Never die   never die
While crying. My lover, my dear one
I will see you next week

When I'm in town. I will call you
If I can. Please get hold of   please don't
Oh God, Please don't any more I can't bear ... Listen:

We have done it again   we are
Still living. Sit up and smile,
God bless you. Guilt is magical.

JUS PRIMAE NOCTIS

Love is a game for only two to play at,
Nor could she banish him from her soft bed
Even on her bridal night, *jus primae noctis*
Being irreversibly his. He took the wall-side
Long ago granted him. Her first-born son
Would claim his name, likeness and character.
Nor did we ask her why. The case was clear:
Even though that lover had been nine years dead
She could not banish him from her soft bed.

SEPARATIONS

Constant Penelope sends to thee, careless Ulysses.
Write not again, but come, sweet mate, thyself to revive me.
Troy we do much envy, we desolate lost ladies of Greece,
Not Priamus, nor yet all Troy can us recompense make.
Oh, that he had, when he first took shipping to Lacedaemon,
That adulter I mean, had been o'erwhelmed with waters.
Then had I not lain now all alone, thus quivering for cold,
Nor used this complaint, nor have thought the day to be so long.

OVID
ANONYMOUS TRANSLATION, 1588

A VALEDICTION: FORBIDDING MOURNING

As virtuous men pass mildly away,
  And whisper to their souls, to go,
Whilst some of their sad friends do say,
  The breath goes now, and some say, no:

So let us melt, and make no noise,
  No tear-floods, nor sigh-tempests move,
'Twere profanation of our joys
  To tell the laity our love.

Moving of th' earth brings harms and fears,
  Men reckon what it did and meant,
But trepidation of the spheres,
  Though greater far, is innocent.

Dull sublunary lovers' love
  (Whose soul is sense) cannot admit
Absence, because it doth remove
  Those things which elemented it.

But we by a love, so much refined,
  That our selves know not what it is,
Inter-assured of the mind,
  Care less, eyes, lips, and hands to miss.

Our two souls therefore, which are one,
    Though I must go, endure not yet
A breach, but an expansion,
    Like gold to aery thinness beat.

If they be two, they are two so
    As stiff twin compasses are two,
Thy soul the fixed foot, makes no show
    To move, but doth, if th' other do.

And though it in the centre sit,
    Yet when the other far doth roam,
It leans, and hearkens after it,
    And grows erect, as that comes home.

Such wilt thou be to me, who must
    Like th' other foot, obliquely run;
Thy firmness makes my circle just,
    And makes me end, where I begun.

LONGING FOR THE EMPEROR

My Lord has departed
And the time has grown long.
Shall I search the mountains,
Going forth to meet you,
Or wait for you here?

No! I would not live,
Longing for you.
On the mountain crag, rather,
Rock-root as my pillow,
Dead would I lie.

Yet even if it be so
I shall wait for my Lord,
Till on my black hair –
Trailing fine in the breeze –
The dawn's frost shall fall.

In the autumn field,
Over the rice ears,
The morning mist trails,
Vanishing somewhere . . .
Can my love fade too?

EMPRESS IWA NO HIME
TRANSLATED BY GEOFFREY BOWNAS
AND ANTHONY THWAITE

THE WORLD AS MEDITATION

J'ai passé trop de temps à travailler mon violon, à voyager.
Mais l'exercice essentiel du compositeur – la méditation –
rien ne l'a jamais suspendu en moi . . . Je vis un rêve
permanent, qui ne s'arrête ni nuit ni jour.

GEORGES ENESCO

Is it Ulysses that approaches from the east,
The interminable adventurer? The trees are mended.
That winter is washed away. Someone is moving

On the horizon and lifting himself up above it.
A form of fire approaches the cretonnes of Penelope,
Whose mere savage presence awakens the world
    in which she dwells.

She has composed, so long, a self with which to
    welcome him,
Companion to his self for her, which she imagined,
Two in a deep-founded sheltering, friend and dear
    friend.

The trees had been mended, as an essential exercise
In an inhuman meditation, larger than her own.
No winds like dogs watched over her at night.

She wanted nothing he could not bring her by coming
 alone.
She wanted no fetchings. His arms would be her
 necklace
And her belt, the final fortune of their desire.

But was it Ulysses? Or was it only the warmth of the
 sun
On her pillow? The thought kept beating in her like
 her heart.
The two kept beating together. It was only day.

It was Ulysses and it was not. Yet they had met,
Friend and dear friend and a planet's encouragement.
The barbarous strength within her would never fail.

She would talk a little to herself as she combed
 her hair,
Repeating his name with its patient syllables,
Never forgetting him that kept coming constantly
 so near.

PARTING

Again, suppose the husband lives in Tzu-yu,
The wife resides in Ho-yang.
They used to share the morning sunlight on their
    jade pendants
And the evening fragrance of the golden incense
    burner.
Now he ties official seals a thousand miles away,
Longing for the precious flower whose fragrance
    is wasted.
She feels guilty about the zither lying idle in her
    chamber,
Darkly on the high terrace the yellow silk curtains
    are drawn.

The spring palace's gates are shut on the green moss,
The autumn curtains are filled with bright moon light;
The summer mats are cool, daylight does not fade,

In the winter lamps the oil thickens, how long
    the night!
As she weaves songs on silk, her tears are all shed;
As she composes revolving-verse poems, alone with
    her shadow she grieves.

      TRANSLATED BY HANS H. FRANKEL

ON LEAVING HIS WIFE

The thick sea-pine
Grows on the rocks
In the sea of Iwami
Off the Cape of Kara.
The sea-tangle clings
To the rocky beach.
Like the sea-tangle
She bent and clung to me,
My wife, my love; deep
As the deep sea-pine
Was my love for her.
Yet the nights are few
When we have slept together.
The creeping ivy parts,
And we have parted too.
My heart aches when I think
Of her, but when I look
Back, the yellow leaves
Of the mountain flutter and hide
Her distant waving sleeve.
As the moon through a wide rift
Peeps, then hides in the clouds,
My wife is hidden, and I
Grieve. The sun is low.
And I, a strong man –

Or so I thought – make wet
My heavy sleeves with tears.
My glossy steed goes fast,
And far as the clouds I've come
From my wife, from my home.
You yellow leaves that cover
The autumn mountain, cease
Your falling for a while,
For I would see my love.

KAKINOMOTO HITOMARO

172 TRANSLATED BY GEOFFREY BOWNAS
AND ANTHONY THWAITE

A LETTER TO HER HUSBAND,
ABSENT UPON PUBLIC EMPLOYMENT

My head, my heart, mine Eyes, my life,
    nay more,
My joy, my Magazine of earthly store,
If two be one, as surely thou and I,
How stayest thou there, whilst I at *Ipswich* lye?
So many steps, head from the heart to sever
If but a neck, soon should we be together:
I like the earth this season, mourn in black,
My Sun is gone so far in's Zodiack,
Whom whilst I 'joy'd, nor storms, nor frosts
     I felt,
His warmth such frigid colds did cause to melt.
My chilled limbs now nummed lye forlorn;
Return, return sweet *Sol* from *Capricorn*;
In this dead time, alas, what can I more
Than view those fruits which through thy heat
     I bore?
Which sweet contentment yield me for a space,
True living Pictures of their Fathers face.
O strange effect! now thou art *Southward* gone,
I weary grow, the tedious day so long;
But when thou *Northward* to me shalt return,
I wish my Sun may never set, but burn
Within the Cancer of my glowing breast,

The welcome house of him my dearest guest.
Where ever, ever stay, and go not thence,
Till natures sad decree shall call thee hence;
Flesh of thy flesh, bone of thy bone,
I here, thou there, yet both but one.

THE RIVER-MERCHANT'S WIFE:
A LETTER

While my hair was still cut straight across my
      forehead
I played about the front gate, pulling flowers.
You came by on bamboo stilts, playing horse,
You walked about my seat, playing with blue plums.
And we went on living in the village of Chokan:
Two small people, without dislike or suspicion.

At fourteen I married My Lord you.
I never laughed, being bashful.
Lowering my head, I looked at the wall.
Called to, a thousand times, I never looked back.

At fifteen I stopped scowling,
I desired my dust to be mingled with yours
For ever and for ever and for ever.
Why should I climb the look out?

At sixteen you departed,
You went into far Ku-to-yen, by the river of swirling
      eddies,
And you have been gone five months.
The monkeys make sorrowful noise overhead.

You dragged your feet when you went out.
By the gate now, the moss is grown, the different
      mosses,
Too deep to clear them away!
The leaves fall early this autumn, in wind.
The paired butterflies are already yellow with August
Over the grass in the West garden;
They hurt me. I grow older.
If you are coming down through the narrows of the
      river Kiang,
Please let me know beforehand,
And I will come out to meet you
            As far as Cho-fu-Sa.

By Rihaku

THE WIFE'S LAMENT

A song I sing   of sorrow unceasing,
The tale of my trouble,   the weight of my woe,
Woe of the present,   and woe of the past,
Woe never-ending   of exile and grief,
But never since girlhood   greater than now.
First, the pang   when my lord departed,
Far from his people,   beyond the sea;
Bitter the heartache   at break of dawn,
The longing for rumor   in what far land
So weary a time   my loved one tarried.
Far I wandered then,   friendless and homeless,
Seeking for help   in my heavy need.

   With secret plotting   his kinsmen purposed
To wedge us apart,   wide worlds between,
And bitter hate.   I was sick at heart.
Harshly my lord   bade lodge me here.
In all this land   I had few to love me,
Few that were loyal,   few that were friends.
Wherefore my spirit   is heavy with sorrow
To learn my beloved,   my dear man and mate
Bowed by ill-fortune   and bitter in heart,
Is masking his purpose   and planning a wrong.
With blithe hearts   often of old we boasted
That nought should part us   save death alone;
All that has failed   and our former love

Is now as if   it had never been!
Far or near   where I fly there follows
The hate of him   who was once so dear.

   In this forest-grove   they have fixed my abode
Under an oak   in a cavern of earth,
An old cave-dwelling   of ancient days,
Where my heart is crushed   by the weight of my woe.
Gloomy its depths   and the cliffs that o'erhang it,
Grim are its confines   with thorns overgrown –
A joyless dwelling   where daily the longing
For an absent loved one   brings anguish of heart.

   Lovers there are   who may live their love,
Joyously keeping   the couch of bliss,
While I in my earth-cave   under the oak
Pace to and fro   in the lonely dawn.
Here must I sit   through the summer-long day,
Here must I weep   in affliction and woe;
Yet never, indeed,   shall my heart know rest
From all its anguish,   and all its ache,
Wherewith life's burdens   have brought me low.

   Ever man's years   are subject to sorrow,
His heart's thoughts bitter,   though his bearing be
      blithe;
Troubled his spirit,   beset with distress –
Whether all wealth   of the world be his lot,
Or hunted by Fate   in a far country
My beloved is sitting   soul-weary and sad,

Swept by the storm,   and stiff with the frost,
In a wretched cell   under rocky cliffs
By severing waters   encircled about –
Sharpest of sorrows   my lover must suffer
Remembering always   a happier home.
Woeful his fate   whose doom is to wait
With longing heart   for an absent love.

ANONYMOUS, ANGLO-SAXON   179
TRANSLATED BY CHARLES W. KENNEDY

PENELOPE IN DOUBT

Forgotten brooch and shrivelled scar,
Were these the only guarantee
This was Odysseus? Did she go
Through twenty years of drifting snow,
Whitening that head and hers, to be
Near as a wife, and yet so far?

The brooch came closer as he told –
Grown suddenly young – how he had lost
The wild doe and the raging hound
That battled in the golden round.
She listened, but what shook her most
Was that these creatures made her old.

Odysseus and that idle tale –
How many things in her had died
While hound and doe shut in the ring
Still fought somewhere in the world, a thing
So strange, her heart knocked on her side.
His eyes with time were bleached and pale.

A stranger, who had seen too much,
Been where she could not follow, sealed
In blank and smooth estranging snow
From head to foot. How could she know
What a brown scar said or concealed?
Yet now she trembled at his touch.

FOR BOTH OF YOU,
THE DIVORCE BEING FINAL

We cannot celebrate with doleful Music
The old, gold panoplies that are so great
To sit and watch; but on the other hand,
To command the nasal krummhorns to be silent,
The *tromba marina* to wail; to have the man
Unlatch the tail gate on his cart, permitting
The sackbut player to extend his slide
And go to work on whimpering divisions;
For us to help prepare the masque itself,
Rigging machinery to collapse the household
Just at the end, rehearsing urchins who
Will trip, all gilded, into the master bedroom
And strip the sheets, is, finally, to confess
That what we lack are rituals adequate
To things like this.

               We tell some anxious friends
'*Basta!* They know what they are doing'; others
Whom we dislike and who, like queens, betray
Never a trace of uneasiness, we play with:
'No, it could never work, my dears, from the start.
We all knew that. Yes, there's the boy to think of,'
And so on. Everyone makes us nervous. Then,
For a dark instant, as in your unlit foyer
At sundown, bringing a parcel, we see you both

And stifle the awkward question: 'What, are *you* here?'
Not because it has been asked before
By Others meeting Underground, but simply
Because we cannot now know which of you
Should answer, or even which of you we asked.
We wait for something to happen in the brown
Shadows around us. Surely there is missing
A tinkle of cymbals to strike up the dirge
And some kind of sounding brass to follow it,
Some hideous and embarrassing gimmick which
Would help us all behave less civilly and
More gently, who mistook civility
So long for lack of gentleness.

                    And since
Weeping's a thing we can no longer manage,
We must needs leave you to the Law's directive:
'You have unmade your bed, now lie about it.'
Quickly now: which of you will keep the *Lares*,
Which the *Penates*? And opening the door
We turn like guilty children, mutter something,
And hide in the twilit street.

                       Along the river
The sky is purpling and signs flash out
And on, to beckon the darkness: THE TIME IS NOW . . .

(What time, what time?) Who stops to look in time
Ever, ever? We can do nothing again
For both of you together. And if I burn
An epithalamium six years old to prove
That what we learn is in some way a function
Of what we forget, I know that I should never
Mention it to anyone. When men
Do in the sunny Plaza what they did
Only in dusky corners before, the sunset
Comes as no benison, the assuring license
Of the June night goes unobserved. The lights
Across the river are brighter than the stars;
The water is black and motionless; whatever
Has happened to all of us, it is too late
For something else ever to happen now.

FOR ANASTASIA'S GRAVE

Alas, alas, the winter of fierce Hell
Bites at the spring of your unnumbered charms;
At the sad age of sixteen the dark tomb
Tore you from sunlight, blinded with fell grief
Your husband and your father for whom you shone
More brightly, Anastasia, than the sun.

IN A LONDON FLAT

I

'You look like a widower,' she said
Through the folding-doors with a laugh from the bed,
As he sat by the fire in the outer room,
Reading late on a night of gloom,
And a cab-hack's wheeze, and the clap of its feet
In its breathless pace on the smooth wet street,
Were all that came to them now and then....
'You really do!' she quizzed again.

II

And the Spirits behind the curtain heard,
And also laughed, amused at her word,
And at her light-hearted view of him.
'Let's get him made so – just for a whim!'
Said the Phantom Ironic. '"Twould serve her right
If we coaxed the Will to do it some night.'
'O pray not!' pleaded the younger one,
The Sprite of the Pities. 'She said it in fun!'

III

But so it befell, whatever the cause,
That what she had called him he next year was;
And on such a night, when she lay elsewhere,
He, watched by those Phantoms, again sat there,
And gazed, as if gazing on far faint shores,
At the empty bed through the folding-doors
As he remembered her words; and wept
That she had forgotten them where she slept.

CORNELIA FROM THE GRAVE
TO HER HUSBAND

Nothing could save me – not our love,
    our marriage,
ancestral glory, our children who mourn today:
they could not keep Cornelia from her dying.
What am I now but dust that a hand could hold?
Black doom and shallow pools of stagnant water
and the streams I walk through, silent and
    icy-cold,
you know I come here innocent and unready . . .

Does ancient lineage gain its recognition?
Africa's conquest was my father's boast;
my mother's family was no less distinguished –
each name upholds our house like a solid post.
I was born to this, and when the wreath of
    marriage
caught up my hair, and I was a woman grown,
it was your bed, my Paullus, that I came to
and now have left. The carving on the stone
says, SHE WED BUT ONCE. O fathers long respected,
victors in Africa, be my defense . . .
and Perseus, proud of great Achilles' kinship
and his who broke through hell's bleak
    battlements:

I asked no favors when Paullus was made censor;
no evil found its way within our walls.
I do not think I have disgraced my fathers;
I set a decent pattern in these halls.
Days had a quiet rhythm; no scandal touched us
from the wedding torch to the torch beside my bier . . .

ON HIS DEAD WIFE

   Sleep on (my Love!) in thy cold bed
Never to be disquieted.
My last Good-night! Thou wilt not wake
Till I Thy Fate shall overtake:
Till age, or grief, or sicknes must
Marry my Body to that Dust
It so much loves; and fill the roome
My heart keepes empty in Thy Tomb.
Stay for mee there: I will not faile
To meet Thee in that hollow Vale.
And think not much of my delay;
I am already on the way,
And follow Thee with all the speed
Desire can make, or Sorrowes breed.
Each Minute is a short Degree
And e'ry Howre a stepp towards Thee.
At Night when I betake to rest,
Next Morne I rise neerer my West
Of Life, almost by eight Howres' sayle,
Then when Sleep breath'd his drowsy gale.
   Thus from the Sunne my Bottome steares,
And my Daye's Compasse downward beares.
Nor labour I to stemme the Tide,
Through which to Thee I swiftly glide.

REUBEN BRIGHT

Because he was a butcher and thereby
Did earn an honest living (and did right),
I would not have you think that Reuben Bright
Was any more a brute than you or I;
For when they told him that his wife must die,
He stared at them, and shook with grief and fright,
And cried like a great baby half that night,
And made the women cry to see him cry.

And after she was dead, and he had paid
The singers and the sexton and the rest,
He packed a lot of things that she had made
Most mournfully away in an old chest
Of hers, and put some chopped-up cedar boughs
In with them, and tore down the slaughter-house.

BENJAMIN PANTIER

Together in this grave lie Benjamin Pantier,
    attorney at law,
And Nig, his dog, constant companion,
    solace and friend.
Down the gray road, friends, children, men and women,
Passing one by one out of life, left me till I was alone
With Nig for partner, bed-fellow, comrade in drink.
In the morning of life I knew aspiration and saw glory.
Then she, who survives me, snared my soul
With a snare which bled me to death,
Till I, once strong of will, lay broken, indifferent,
Living with Nig in a room back of a dingy office.
Under my jaw-bone is snuggled the bony nose of Nig –
Our story is lost in silence. Go by, mad world!

MRS. BENJAMIN PANTIER

I know that he told that I snared his soul
With a snare which bled him to death.
And all the men loved him,
And most of the women pitied him.
But suppose you are really a lady, and have delicate
     tastes,
And loathe the smell of whiskey and onions.
And the rhythm of Wordsworth's 'Ode' runs in
     your ears,
While he goes about from morning till night
Repeating bits of that common thing,
'Oh, why should the spirit of mortal be proud?'
And then, suppose:
You are a woman well endowed,
And the only man with whom the law and morality
Permit you to have the marital relation
Is the very man that fills you with disgust
Every time you think of it – while you think of it
Every time you see him?
That's why I drove him away from home
To live with his dog in a dingy room
Back of his office.

A WIDOW'S HYMN

How near me came the hand of Death,
　　When at my side he struck my dear,
And took away the precious breath
　　Which quickened my belovèd peer!
　　　　How helpless am I thereby made!
　　　　By day how grieved, by night how sad!
And now my life's delight is gone,
Alas! how am I left alone!

The voice which I did more esteem
　　Than music in her sweetest key,
Those eyes which unto me did seem
　　More comfortable than the day;
　　　　Those now by me, as they have been,
　　　　Shall never more be heard or seen;
But what I once enjoyed in them
Shall seem hereafter as a dream.

Lord! keep me faithful to the trust
　　Which my dear spouse reposed in me:
To him now dead preserve me just
　　In all that should performèd be!
　　　　For though our being man and wife
　　　　Extendeth only to this life,
Yet neither life nor death should end
The being of a faithful friend.

194　GEORGE WITHER

THE SONG OF THE WIDOW

In the beginning life was good to me.
It held me warmly, it gave me heart.
Of course it does that to all the young,
but back then how could I know?
I didn't know what living was –,
suddenly it was only year and year,
no longer bright, no longer fine, no longer
        magical,
as if ripped right in two.

It wasn't his, it wasn't my fault,
we both had nothing except patience,
but Death had none.
I saw him come (how meanly!)
and I watched him as he took and took:
none of it I could claim as mine.

What, then, *was* mine: mine, my own?
Was even my core of wretchedness
only lent to me by fate?
Fate wants not only the happiness,
it wants the pain and screaming back,
and it buys the ruin second-hand.

Fate was there and obtained for a pittance
every expression of my face,
even the way I walk.
That was a daily close-out sale,
and when I was empty, it gave me up
and left me standing open.

THE WIDOWER

For a season there must be pain –
For a little, little space
I shall lose the sight of her face,
Take back the old life again
While She is at rest in her place.

For a season this pain must endure,
For a little, little while
I shall sigh more often than smile
Till Time shall work me a cure,
And the pitiful days beguile.

For that season we must be apart,
For a little length of years,
Till my life's last hour nears,
And, above the beat of my heart,
I hear Her voice in my ears.

But I shall not understand –
Being set on some later love,
Shall not know her for whom I strove,
Till she reach me forth her hand,
Saying, 'Who but I have the right?'
And out of a troubled night
Shall draw me safe to the land.

RUDYARD KIPLING   197

THE WIDOW'S SONG

I burn no incense, hang no wreath,
    On this, thine early tomb:
Such cannot cheer the place of death,
    But only mock its gloom.
Here odorous smoke and breathing flower
    No grateful influence shed;
They lose their perfume and their power,
    When offered to the dead.

And if, as is the Afghaun's creed,
    The spirit may return,
A disembodied sense to feed,
    On fragrance, near its urn –
It is enough, that she, whom thou
    Did'st love in living years,
Sits desolate beside it now,
    And falls these heavy tears.

COMPLAINT

She's gone. She was my love, my moon or more.
She chased the chickens out and swept the floor,
Emptied the bones and nut-shells after feasts,
And smacked the kids for leaping up like beasts.
Now morbid boys have grown past awkwardness;
The girls let stitches out, dress after dress,
To free some swinging body's riding space
And form the new child's unimagined face.
Yet, while vague nephews, spitting on their curls,
Amble to pester winds and blowsy girls,
What arm will sweep the room, what hand will hold
New snow against the milk to keep it cold?
And who will dump the garbage, feed the hogs,
And pitch the chickens' heads to hungry dogs?
Not my lost hag who dumbly bore such pain:
Childbirth and midnight sassafras and rain.
New snow against her face and hands she bore,
And now lies down, who was my moon or more.

OVER THE COFFIN

They stand confronting, the coffin between,
His wife of old, and his wife of late,
And the dead man whose they both had been
Seems listening aloof, as to things past date.
— 'I have called,' says the first. 'Do you marvel or not?'
'In truth,' says the second, 'I do — somewhat.'

'Well, there was a word to be said by me! . . .
I divorced that man because of you —
It seemed I must do it, boundenly;
But now I am older, and tell you true,
For life is little, and dead lies he;
I would I had let alone you two!
And both of us, scorning the parochial ways,
Had lived like the wives in the patriarchs' days.'

METHOUGHT...

Methought I saw my late espoused saint
    Brought to me like Alcestis from the grave,
    Whom Jove's great son to her glad husband gave,
    Rescued from death by force though pale and faint.
Mine as whom washed from spot of childbed taint,
    Purification in the old Law did save,
    And such, as yet once more I trust to have
    Full sight of her in heaven without restraint,
Came vested all in white, pure as her mind:
    Her face was veiled, yet to my fancied sight,
    Love, sweetness, goodness in her person shined
So clear, as in no face with more delight.
    But O as to embrace me she inclined
    I waked, she fled, and day brought back my night.

JOHN MILTON

SYMBOLIC
MARRIAGES

. . . the sun
Which is as a bridegroom coming out of his chamber

PSALM 19

LIFE IS MOTION

In Oklahoma,
Bonnie and Josie,
Dressed in calico,
Danced around a stump.
They cried,
'Ohoyaho,
Ohoo' ...
Celebrating the marriage
Of flesh and air.

THE MARRIAGE OF EARTH AND HEAVEN

Earth draws her breath so gently, heaven bends
On her so bright a look, I could believe
That the renewal of the world was come,
The marriage of kind Earth and splendid Heaven.

'O happy pair' – the blind man lifts his harp
Down from the peg – but wait, but check the song.
The two you praise still matchless lie apart,
Thin air drawn sharp between queen Earth and
     Heaven.

Though I stand and stretch my hands forever
Till my hair grows down my back and my skirt to my
     ankles,
I shall not hear the triumphs of their trumpets
Calling the hopeful in from all the quarters
To the marriage of kind Earth and splendid Heaven.

Yet out of reason's reach a place is kept
For great occasions, with a fat four-poster bed
And a revelling-ground and a fountain showering beer
And a fiddler fiddling fine for folly's children
To riot rings around at the famous wedding
Of quean Earth and her fancy-fellow Heaven.

THE WORLD STANDS
SOLEMNER TO ME

The World – stands – solemner – to me –
Since I was wed – to Him –
A modesty befits the soul
That bears another's – name –
A doubt – if it be fair – indeed –
To wear that perfect – pearl –
The Man – upon the Woman – binds –
To clasp her soul – for all –
A prayer, that it more angel – prove –
A whiter Gift – within –
To that munificence, that chose –
So unadorned – a Queen –
A Gratitude – that such be true –
It had esteemed the Dream –
Too beautiful – for Shape to prove –
Or posture – to redeem!

A NEW WIFE

You know, my Friends, how bravely in my
    House
For a new Marriage I did make Carouse;
   Divorced old barren Reason from my
    Bed,
And took the Daughter of the Vine to
    Spouse

MARRIED SOUNDS

Music to hear, why hear'st thou music sadly?
Sweets with sweets war not, joy delights in joy.
Why lov'st thou that which thou receiv'st not gladly,
Or else receiv'st with pleasure thine annoy?
If the true concord of well tunèd sounds,
By unions married, do offend thine ear,
They do but sweetly chide thee, who confounds
In singleness the parts that thou shouldst bear.
Mark how one string, sweet husband to another,
Strikes each in each by mutual ordering;
Resembling sire, and child, and happy mother,
Who all in one, one pleasing note do sing;
   Whose speechless song, being many, seeming one,
    Sings this to thee, 'Thou single wilt prove none.'

WILLIAM SHAKESPEARE

SOUTH GARDEN

Flower branches and grass stems blossom before
    the eye,
Little white and long red: cheeks of a girl from Yüeh.
What a pity that at Sundown the charming fragrance
    falls.
For her wedding with the spring wind, no fragrance
    was employed.

      TRANSLATED BY HANS H. FRANKEL

JANE'S MARRIAGE
'THE JANEITES'

Jane went to Paradise:
　　That was only fair.
Good Sir Walter followed her,
　　And armed her up the stair.
Henry and Tobias,
　　And Miguel of Spain,
Stood with Shakespeare at the top
　　To welcome Jane –

Then the Three Archangels
　　Offered out of hand
Anything in Heaven's gift
　　That she might command.
Azrael's eyes upon her,
　　Raphael's wings above,
Michael's sword against her heart,
　　Jane said: 'Love.'

Instantly the under-
　　standing Seraphim
Laid their fingers on their lips
　　And went to look for him.
Stole across the Zodiac,

Harnessed Charles's Wain,
And whispered round the Nebulæ
'Who loved Jane?'

In a private limbo
    Where none had thought to look,
Sat a Hampshire gentleman
    Reading of a book.
It was called *Persuasion*,
    And it told the plain
Story of the love between
    Him and Jane.

He heard the question
    Circle Heaven through –
Closed the book and answered:
    'I did – and do!'
Quietly but speedily
    (As Captain Wentworth moved)
Entered into Paradise
    The man Jane loved!

Jane lies in Winchester, blessèd be her shade!
Praise the Lord for making her, and her for all she made.
And, while the stones of Winchester – or Milsom Street –
        remain,
Glory, Love, and Honour unto England's Jane!

FOR A MARRIAGE OF ST. CATHERINE
BY MEMLING

Mystery: Catherine the bride of Christ.
   She kneels, and on her hand the holy Child
   Now sets the ring. Her life is hushed and mild,
Laid in God's knowledge – ever unenticed
From God, and in the end thus fitly priced.
   Awe, and the music that is near her, wrought
   Of angels, have possessed her eyes in thought:
Her utter joy is hers, and hath sufficed.

There is a pause while Mary Virgin turns
   The leaf, and reads. With eyes on the spread book,
     That damsel at her knees reads after her.
     John whom He loved, and John His harbinger,
   Listen and watch. Whereon soe'er thou look,
The light is starred in gems and the gold burns.

DANTE GABRIEL ROSSETTI

TITLE DIVINE

Title divine – is mine!
The Wife – without the Sign!
Acute Degree – conferred on me –
Empress of Calvary!
Royal – all but the Crown!
Betrothed – without the swoon
God sends us Women –
When you – hold – Garnet to Garnet –
Gold – to Gold –
Born – Bridalled – Shrouded –
In a Day –
Tri Victory
'My Husband' – women say
Stroking the Melody –
Is *this* – the way?

FOR AND AGAINST MARRIAGE

I would be married, but I'de have no Wife,
I would be married to a single Life.

RICHARD CRASHAW

Riches of children passe a Prince's throne;
Which touch the father's hart with secret joy,
When with shame he saith, 'these be mine owne'.
Marrie therefore; for marriage will destroy
Those passions which to youthfull head doo clime,
Mothers and Nurses of all vaine annoy.

SIR PHILIP SIDNEY

When a Man has married a Wife he finds out whether
Her knees and elbows are only glued together.

WILLIAM BLAKE

'NO CAUSE OR JUST IMPEDIMENT'

Let me not to the marriage of true minds
Admit impediments; love is not love
Which alters when it alteration finds,
Or bends with the remover to remove.
O, no, it is an ever-fixèd mark
That looks on tempests and is never shaken;
It is the star to every wand'ring bark,
Whose worth's unknown, although his height be
    taken.
Love's not Time's fool, though rosy lips and cheeks
Within his bending sickle's compass come;
Love alters not with his brief hours and weeks,
But bears it out even to the edge of doom.
   If this be error and upon me proved,
   I never writ, nor no man ever loved.

THE DREARIEST JOURNEY

I never was attached to that great sect,
Whose doctrine is, that each one should select
Out of the crowd a mistress or a friend,
And all the rest, though fair and wise, commend
To cold oblivion, though it is the code
Of modern morals, and the beaten road
Which those poor slaves with weary footsteps tread,
By the broad highway of the world, and so
With one chained friend, perhaps a jealous foe,
The dreariest and the longest journey go.

TO THE VIRGINS,
TO MAKE MUCH OF TIME

Gather ye Rose-buds while ye may,
   Old Time is still a flying:
And this same flower that smiles today,
   To morrow will be dying.

The glorious Lamp of Heaven, the Sun,
   The higher he's a getting;
The sooner will his Race be run,
   And neerer he's to Setting.

That Age is best, which is the first,
   When Youth and Blood are warmer;
But being spent, the worse, and worst
   Times, still succeed the former.

Then be not coy, but use your time;
   And while ye may, goe marry:
For having lost but once your prime,
   You may for ever tarry.

THE REAL AND TRUE AND SURE

Marriage on earth seems such a counterfeit,
Mere imitation of the inimitable:
In heaven we have the real and true and sure.
'T is there they neither marry nor are given
In marriage but are as the angels: right,
Oh how right that is, how like Jesus Christ
To say that! Marriage-making for the earth,
With gold so much, – birth, power, repute so much,
Or beauty, youth so much, in lack of these!
Be as the angels rather, who, apart,
Know themselves into one, are found at length
Married, but marry never, no, nor give
In marriage; they are man and wife at once
When the true time is: here we have to wait
Not so long neither! Could we by a wish
Have what we will and get the future now,
Would we wish aught done undone in the past?
So, let him wait God's instant men call years;
Meantime hold hard by truth and his great soul,
Do out the duty! Through such souls alone
God stooping shows sufficient of His light
For us i' the dark to rise by. And I rise.

THE NEED OF POSTERITY

Look in thy glass and tell the face thou viewest
Now is the time that face should form another,
Whose fresh repair if now thou not renewest,
Thou dost beguile the world, unbless some mother.
For where is she so fair whose uneared womb
Disdains the tillage of thy husbandry?
Or who is he so fond will be the tomb
Of his self-love to stop posterity?
Thou art thy mother's glass, and she in thee
Calls back the lovely April of her prime;
So thou through windows of thine age shalt see,
Despite of wrinkles, this thy golden time.
    But if thou live rememb'red not to be,
      Die single and thine image dies with thee.

A WORD AGAINST WIVES

Shrewdnes so stirres, pride so puffes up their hart,
They seldome ponder what to them is due.
  With meager lookes, as if they still did smart;
Puiling, and whimpring, or else scolding flat,
Make home more paine then following of the cart.
  Either dull silence, or eternall chat;
Still contrarie to what her husband sayes;
If he do praise the dog, she likes the cat.
  Austere she is, when he would honest playes;
And gamesome then, when he thinkes on his sheepe;
She bids him goe, and yet from jorney stayes.
  She warre doth ever with his kinsfolke keepe,
And makes them fremb'd, who frendes by nature are,
Envying shallow toyes with malice deepe.
  And if forsooth there come some new found ware,
The little coine his sweating browes have got,
Must goe for that, if for her lowres he care:
  Or els; 'Nay faith, mine is the lucklest lot,
That ever fell to honest woman yet:
No wife but I hath such a man, God wot'.
  Such is their speech, who be of sober wit;
But who doo let their tongues shew well their rage,
Lord, what bywords they speake, what spite they spit?
  The house is made a very lothsome cage,
Wherein the birde doth never sing but cry...

WASTED BEAUTY

Is it for fear to wet a widow's eye
That thou consum'st thyself in single life?
Ah, if thou issueless shalt hap to die,
The world will wail thee like a makeless wife;
The world will be thy widow and still weep,
That thou no form of thee hast left behind,
When every private widow well may keep,
By children's eyes, her husband's shape in mind.
Look what an unthrift in the world doth spend,
Shifts but his place, for still the world enjoys it;
But beauty's waste hath in the world an end,
And kept unused, the user so destroys it:
    No love toward others in that bosom sits
    That on himself such murd'rous shame commits.

WARNING TO A WIFE

Either get out of the house or conform to my tastes,
    woman.
I'm no strait-laced old Roman.
I like prolonging the nights agreeably with wine: you,
    after one glass of water,
Rise and retire with an air of hauteur.
You prefer darkness: I enjoy love-making
With a witness – a lamp shining or the dawn breaking.
You wear bed-jackets, tunics, thick woollen stuff,
Whereas I think no woman on her back can ever be
    naked enough.
I love girls who kiss like doves and hang round
    my neck:
You give me the sort of peck
Due to your grandmother as a morning salute.
In bed, you're motionless, mute –
Not a wriggle,
Not a giggle –
As solemn as a priestess at a shrine
Proffering incense and pure wine.
Yet every time Andromache went for a ride
In Hector's room, the household slaves used to
    masturbate outside;
Even modest Penelope, when Ulysses snored,
Kept her hand on the sceptre of her lord.

You refuse to be buggered; but it's a known fact
That Gracchus', Pompey's and Brutus' wives were
    willing partners in the act,
And that before Ganymede mixed Jupiter his tasty
    bowl
Juno filled the dear boy's role.
If you want to be uptight – all right,
By all means play Lucretia by day. But I need a Laïs
    at night.

MARTIAL

TRANSLATED BY JAMES MICHIE

THE MARRIAGE OF SOULS

That heat!
That terrible heat
That coldness!
That terrible coldness

Alone!
At the flame's tip
Alone!
In the sparkling crystal

So they stay
Adjacent
Like to like
In terrible isolation

Like to like
In terrible intimacy
Unfused
And unfusing

MARRIAGE

Should I get married? Should I be good?
Astound the girl next door with my velvet suit and
 faustus hood?
Don't take her to movies but to cemeteries
tell all about werewolf bathtubs and forked clarinets
then desire her and kiss her and all the preliminaries
and she going just so far and I understanding why
not getting angry saying You must feel! It's beautiful to
 feel!
Instead take her in my arms lean against an old crooked
 tombstone
and woo her the entire night the constellations in the sky –

When she introduces me to her parents
back straightened, hair finally combed, strangled
 by a tie,
should I sit knees together on their 3rd degree sofa
and not ask Where's the bathroom?
How else to feel other than I am,
often thinking Flash Gordon soap –
O how terrible it must be for a young man
seated before a family and the family thinking
We never saw him before! He wants our Mary Lou!
After tea and homemade cookies they ask What do you
 do for a living?

Should I tell them? Would they like me then?
Say All right get married, we're losing a daughter
but we're gaining a son –
And should I then ask Where's the bathroom?

O God, and the wedding! All her family and her friends
and only a handful of mine all scroungy and bearded
just wait to get at the drinks and food –
And the priest! he looking at me as if I masturbated
asking me Do you take this woman for your lawful
          wedded wife?
And I trembling what to say say Pie Glue!
I kiss the bride all those corny men slapping me
          on the back
She's all yours, boy! Ha-ha-ha!
And in their eyes you could see some obscene
          honeymoon going on –
Then all that absurd rice and clanky cans and shoes
Niagara Falls! Hordes of us! Husbands! Wives!
          Flowers! Chocolates!
All streaming into cozy hotels
All going to do the same thing tonight
The indifferent clerk he knowing what was going
          to happen
The lobby zombies they knowing what
The whistling elevator man he knowing
The winking bellboy knowing

Everybody knowing! I'd be almost inclined not to do
        anything!
Stay up all night! Stare that hotel clerk in the eye!
Screaming: I deny honeymoon! I deny honeymoon!
running rampant into those almost climactic suites
yelling Radio belly! Cat shovel!
O I'd live in Niagara forever! in a dark cave beneath
        the Falls
I'd sit there the Mad Honeymooner
devising ways to break marriages, a scourge of bigamy
a saint of divorce –

But I should get married I should be good
How nice it'd be to come home to her
and sit by the fireplace and she in the kitchen
aproned young and lovely wanting my baby
and so happy about me she burns the roast beef
and comes crying to me and I get up from my
        big papa chair
saying Christmas teeth! Radiant brains! Apple deaf!
God what a husband I'd make! Yes, I should get married!
So much to do! like sneaking into Mr Jones' house late
        at night
and cover his golf clubs with 1920 Norwegian books
Like hanging a picture of Rimbaud on the lawnmower
like pasting Tannu Tuva postage stamps all over the
        picket fence

229

like when Mrs Kindhead comes to collect for the
        Community Chest
grab her and tell her There are unfavorable omens
        in the sky!
And when the mayor comes to get my vote tell him
When are you going to stop people killing whales!
And when the milkman comes leave him a note
        in the bottle
Penguin dust, bring me penguin dust, I want penguin
        dust –

Yet if I should get married and it's Connecticut and
        snow
and she gives birth to a child and I am sleepless,
        worn,
up for nights, head bowed against a quiet window,
        the past behind me,
finding myself in the most common of situations
        a trembling man
knowledged with responsibility not twig-smear
        nor Roman coin soup –
O what would that be like!
Surely I'd give it for a nipple a rubber Tacitus
For a rattle a bag of broken Bach records
Tack Della Francesca all over its crib
Sew the Greek alphabet on its bib
And build for its playpen a roofless Parthenon

No, I doubt I'd be that kind of father
not rural not snow no quiet window
but hot smelly tight New York City
seven flights up, roaches and rats in the walls
a fat Reichian wife screeching over potatoes Get a job!
And five nose running brats in love with Batman
And the neighbors all toothless and dry haired
like those hag masses of the 18th century
all wanting to come in and watch TV
The landlord wants his rent
Grocery store Blue Cross Gas & Electric Knights
    of Columbus
Impossible to lie back and dream Telephone snow,
    ghost parking –
No! I should not get married I should never
    get married!
But – imagine If I were married to a beautiful
    sophisticated woman
tall and pale wearing an elegant black dress and long
    black gloves
holding a cigarette holder in one hand and a highball
    in the other
and we lived high up in a penthouse with a huge window
from which we could see all of New York and ever
    farther on clearer days
No, can't imagine myself married to that pleasant
    prison dream –

O but what about love? I forget love
not that I am incapable of love
it's just that I see love as odd as wearing shoes –
I never wanted to marry a girl who was like my mother
And Ingrid Bergman was always impossible
And there's maybe a girl now but she's already married
And I don't like men and –
but there's got to be somebody!
Because what if I'm 60 years old and not married,
all alone in a furnished room with pee stains on my
        underwear
and everybody else is married! All the universe
        married but me!

Ah, yet well I know that were a woman possible as I am
        possible
then marriage would be possible –
Like SHE in her lonely alien gaud waiting her
        Egyptian lover
so I wait – bereft of 2,000 years and the bath of life.

CALL IT A GOOD MARRIAGE

Call it a good marriage –
For no one ever questioned
Her warmth, his masculinity,
Their interlocking views;
Except one stray graphologist
Who frowned in speculation
At her h's and her s's,
His p's and w's.

Though few would still subscribe
To the monogramic axiom
That strife below the hip-bones
Need not estrange the heart,
Call it a good marriage:
More drew those two together,
Despite a lack of children,
Than pulled them apart.

Call it a good marriage:
They never fought in public,
They acted circumspectly
And faced the world with pride;
Thus the hazards of their love-bed
Were none of our damned business –
Till as jurymen we sat upon
Two deaths by suicide.

ROBERT GRAVES

TOWARD A DEFINITION OF MARRIAGE

I

It is to make a fill, not find a land.
Elsewhere, often, one sights americas of awareness,
suddenly there they are, natural and anarchic,
with plantings scattered but rich, powers to be
    harnessed –
but this is more like building a World's Fair island.
Somebody thought it could be done, contracts are signed,
and now all materials are useful, everything; sludge
is scooped up and mixed with tin cans and fruit rinds,
even tomato pulp and lettuce leaves are solid
under pressure. Presently the ground humps up
    and shows.
But this marvel of engineering is not all.
A hodgepodge of creatures (no bestiary would suppose
such an improbable society) are at this time
turned loose to run on it, first shyly, then more free,
and must keep, for self's sake, wiles, anger, much of
    their
spiney or warted nature, yet learn courtesy.

II

It is closest to picaresque, but essentially artless.
If there were any experts, they are dead, it takes
    too long.

How could its structure be more than improvising,
when it never ends, but line after line plods on,
and none of the ho hum passages can be skipped?
It has a bulky knowledge, but what symbol comes
     anywhere near
suggesting it? No, the notion of art won't fit it –
unless – when it's embodied. For digression there
is meaningful, and takes such joy in the slopes and
     crannies
that every bony gesture is generous, full,
all lacy with veins and nerves. There, the spirit
smiles in its skin, and impassions and sweetens to style.
So this comes to resemble a poem found in his
     notebooks
after the master died. A charred, balky man, yet one day
as he worked at one of those monuments, the sun guiled
     him,
and he turned to a fresh page and simply let play
his great gift on a small ground. Yellowed, unpublished,
he might have forgotten he wrote it. (All this is
     surmise.)
But it's known by heart now; it rounded the steeliest
     shape
to shapeliness, it was so loving an exercise.

Or, think of it as a duel of amateurs.
These two have almost forgot how it started – in an
    alley,
impromptu, and with a real affront. One thought,
'He is not me,' and one, 'She is not me,'
and they were coming toward each other with sharp
    knives
when someone saw it was illegal, dragged them away,
bundled them into some curious canvas clothing,
and brought them to this gym that is almost dark,
    and empty.
Now, too close together for the length of the foils,
wet with fear, they dodge, stumble, strike,
and if either finally thinks he would rather be touched
than touch, he still must listen to the clang and tick
of his own compulsive parrying. Endless. Nothing
but a scream for help can make the authorities come.
If it ever turns into more of a dance than a duel,
it is only because, feeling more skillful, one
or the other steps back with some notion of grace
and looks at his partner. Then he is able to find
not a wire mask for his target, but a red heart
sewn on the breast like a simple valentine.

IV

If there's a Barnum way to show it, then think back
to a climax in the main tent. At the foot of the
        bleachers, a road
encloses the ringed acts; consider that as its design,
and consider whoever undertakes it as the whole parade
which, either as preview or summary, assures the
        public
hanging in hopeful suspense between balloons and
        peanutshells
that it's all worthwhile. The ponies never imagined
anything but this slow trot of ribbons and jinglebells.
An enormous usefulness constrains the leathery bulls
as they stomp on, and hardly ever run amuck.
The acrobats practised all their lives for this easy
contortion, and clowns are enacting a necessary joke
by harmless zigzags in and out of line.
But if the procession includes others less trustworthy?
When they first see the circle they think some ignorant
cartographer has blundered. The route is a lie,
drawn to be strict but full, drawn so each going forth
returns, returns to a more informed beginning.
And still a familiar movement might tempt them to try it,
but since what they know is not mentioned in the
        tromboning
of the march, neither the day-long pace of caged
impulse, nor the hurtle of night's terrible box-cars,

they shrink in their stripes and refuse; other performers
drive them out and around with whips and chairs.
They never tame, but may be taught to endure
the illusion of tameness. Year after year their paws
pad out the false curve, and their reluctant parading
extends the ritual's claim to its applause.

v

Say, for once, that the start is a pure vision
like the blind man's (though he couldn't keep it, trees
soon bleached to familiar) when the bandage came off
and what a world could be first fell on his eyes.
Say it's when campaigns are closest to home
that farsighted lawmakers oftenest lose their way.
And repeat what everyone knows and nobody wants
to remember, that always, always expediency
must freckle the fairest wishes. Say, when documents,
stiff with history, go right into the council chambers
and are rolled up to shake under noses, are constantly
    read from,
or pounded on, or passed around, the parchment
    limbers;
and, still later, if these old papers are still being
    shuffled,
commas will be missing, ashes will disfigure a word;
finally thumbprints will grease out whole phrases,
    the clear prose

won't mean much; it can never be wholly restored.
Curators mourn the perfect idea, for it crippled
outside of its case. Announce that at least it can move
in the imperfect action, beyond the windy oratory,
of marriage, which is the politics of love.

THE WAY THINGS ARE

Women conceive more readily, if taken
As animals are, breasts underneath, loins high,
So that the seed reaches the proper parts
More readily. Wives have no need at all
For loose and limber motions, pelvic stunts,
Abdominal gyrations. These, in fact,
Are contraceptive; if she pulls away,
Pretends reluctance, stirs him up again
With strain and push and thrusting, she diverts
The seed from its right furrow. This is why
All whores are so gymnastic; they know well
Such acts not only please their customers
But also are a safeguard, good insurance
Against a pregnant belly. But our wives,
It seems, need no such nonsense. Finally,
The little woman does not have to be
A raving beauty; she can win your love,
Without the help of any gods, without
The darts of Cupids or of Venuses,
Simply by being decent, neat and clean,
A pleasant person to be living with.
That's about all it takes, and love depends
On habit quite as much as the wild ways
Of passion. Gently does it, as the rain
In time wears through the very hardest stone.

TRANSLATED BY ROLFE HUMPHRIES

MARRIAGES

When those of us who seem
Immodestly-accurate
Transcriptions of a dream
Are tired of singleness,
Their confidence will mate
Only with confidence –
With an equal candescence,
With a pregnant selfishness.

Not so with the remainder:
Frogmarched by old need
They chaffer for a partner –
Some undesirable,
With whom it is agreed
That words such as liberty,
Impulse, or beauty
Shall be unmentionable.

Scarecrows of chivalry
They strike strange bargains –
Adder-faced singularity
Espouses a nailed-up childhood,
Skin-disease pardons
Soft horror of living,
A gabble is forgiven
By chronic solitude.

So they are gathered in;
So they are not wasted,
As they would have been
By intelligent rancour,
An integrity of self-hatred.
Whether they forget
What they wanted first or not
They tarnish at quiet anchor.

ACKNOWLEDGMENTS

Thanks are due to the following copyright holders for permission to reprint:

CHIANG YEN: 'Parting' by Chiang Yen from Hans H. Frankel *The Flowering Plum and the Palace Lady* published by Yale University Press. CORSO, GREGORY: 'Marriage' by Gregory Corso from *The Happy Birthday of Death*. Copyright © 1960 by New Directions Publishing Corp. Reprinted by permission of New Directions Publishing Corp. CUNNINGHAM, J. V.: 'To My Wife' by J. V. Cunningham, from *Collected Poems and Epigrams of J. V. Cunningham*. Reprinted with the permission of Ohio University Press/Swallow Press, Athens. DICKEY, JAMES: 'Adultery' from *Poems 1957–1967* © 1966 Wesleyan University Press by permission University Press of New England. DICKINSON, EMILY: 'Title Divine', Poem No. 1072 from *Life and Letters of Emily Dickinson*, edited by Martha Dickinson Bianchi. Copyright 1924 by Martha Dickinson Bianchi, © renewed 1952 by Alfred Leete Hampson. Reprinted by permission of Houghton Mifflin Company. All rights reserved. FROST, ROBERT: 'The Telephone' and 'The Hill Wife' from *The Poetry of Robert Frost* edited by Edward Connery Lathem published by Jonathan Cape reprinted by permission of

246

INDEX OF AUTHORS

ANONYMOUS:

    I Shall Be Married on Monday Morning ..   17

    Her Father's House   24

    Lord Thomas and Fair Eleanor   46

    The Frog and the Mouse   49

    For Poorer   81

    The Wraggle Taggle Gipsies   146

    My Mother Made Me Marry   148

    The Flower-Girl   150

    The Wife's Lament   177

WILLIAM BARNES (1801–86): Jeäne   132

THE BIBLE:

    The Bride Sings (*from* The Song of Songs)   43

SAMUEL BISHOP (1731–95): A Second Ring   130

ANNE BRADSTREET (?1613–72):

    Before the Birth of One of Her Children ..   107

    A Letter to Her Husband, Absent upon

        Public Employment   173

RUPERT BROOKE (1887–1915):

    Menelaus and Helen   144

ROBERT BROWNING (1812–89):

    My Last Duchess   32

    The Householder   119

    The Real and True and Sure   220

ROBERT BURNS (1759–96): John Anderson My Jo   139

THOMAS CAMPION (1567–1620):
    Song ('Now hath *Flora* rob'd her bowers') ..   72
CHIANG YEN (AD 444–505): Parting   170
ARTHUR HUGH CLOUGH (1819–61):
    Silver Wedding   127
GREGORY CORSO (1930–): Marriage   227
RICHARD CRASHAW (1613?–49):
    Harmony   71
    An Epitaph upon Husband and Wife Who
        Died and Were Buried Together   140
J. V. CUNNINGHAM (1911–85): To My Wife   138
JAMES DICKEY (1923–): Adultery   160
EMILY DICKINSON (1839–86):
    The World Stands Solemner to Me   207
    Title Divine   214
JOHN DONNE (1572–1631):
    Ceremonials   51
    A Valediction: Forbidding Mourning   165
JOHN DRYDEN (1631–1700):
    A Foolish Marriage Vow   143
ROBERT FROST (1874–1963):
    The Telephone   110
    The Hill Wife   115
ROBERT GRAVES (1895–1985):
    Jus Primae Noctis   162
    Call It a Good Marriage   233
RACHEL HADAS (1948–): *From* Love   94

MOISHE LEIB HALPERN (1896–1932): The Marriage   87

THOMAS HARDY (1840–1928):

    The Wedding Morning   42

    At the Altar-Rail   58

    A Beauty's Soliloquy during Her Honeymoon   69

    At the Dinner-Table   82

    A Question of Marriage   84

    She Revisits Alone the Church of Her

        Marriage   96

    At Tea   105

    In the Restaurant   154

    In a London Flat   186

    Over the Coffin   200

ROBERT HERRICK (1591–1674):

    Upon One Lillie, Who Married with a Maid

        Call'd Rose   88

    Upon Jolly and Jilly   111

    To the Virgins, to Make Much of Time   . .   219

JOHN HOLLANDER (1929–):

    For Both of You, the Divorce Being Final   . .   182

EMPRESS IWA NO HIME (d. AD 347):

    Longing for the Emperor   167

JULIAN (PREFECT OF EGYPT) (*fl.* early 5th century):

    For Anastasia's Grave   185

DONALD JUSTICE (1925–): On an Anniversary   . .   133

KAKINOMOTO HITOMARO (d. AD 708):

    On Leaving His Wife   171

OMAR KHAYYÁM (d. 1022 or 1032):

    A New Wife 208

HENRY KING (1592–1669):

    On his Dead Wife 190

RUDYARD KIPLING (1865–1936):

    Harp Song of the Dane Women 156

    The Widower 197

    Jane's Marriage 211

PHILIP LARKIN (1922–85):

    Wedding-Wind 74

    Marriages 241

D. H. LAWRENCE (1885–1930):

    Wedding Morn . . . . , . . 40

    The Painter's Wife . . . . , 86

EDWARD LEAR (1812–88):

    The Owl and the Pussy-Cat 30

LI HO (AD 791–817): South Garden 210

HENRY WADSWORTH LONGFELLOW (1807–82):

    Hiawatha's Wedding-Feast 54

ROBERT LOWELL (1917–77):

    'To Speak of Woe That Is in Marriage' . . 106

LUCAN [MARCUS ANNAEUS LUCANUS] (AD 39–65):

    For a Remarriage 59

LUCRETIUS [TITUS LUCRETIUS CARUS] (99?–50? BC):

    The Way Things Are 240

JAY MacPHERSON (1931–):

    The Marriage of Earth and Heaven . . . 206

MARTIAL (AD 40–103/4): Warning to a Wife . . 224
EDGAR LEE MASTERS (1868–1950):
    Benjamin Pantier 192
    Mrs. Benjamin Pantier 193
GEORGE MEREDITH (1928–1909):
    Love in the Valley 26
    Modern Marriage 112
    Guests for Dinner 155
    The Triangle 158
JAMES MERRILL (1926–95):
    Upon a Second Marriage 60
EDNA ST. VINCENT MILLAY (1892–1950):
    The Betrothal 35
    Witch-Wife 114
JOHN MILTON (1608–74):
    Discourse 109
    Methought 201
EDWIN MUIR (1887–1959):
    The Commemoration 136
    Penelope in Doubt 180
MUSAEUS [?5th century AD):
    The Marriage of Hero and Leander 45
OVID (43 BC–AD 17):
    The Story of Baucis and Philemon 89
    The Art of Deceiving a Husband 151
EDWARD COOTE PINKNEY (1802–28):
    The Widow's Song 198

EZRA POUND (1885–1972):

    The River-Merchant's Wife: A Letter 175

MATTHEW PRIOR (1664–1721):

    To a Friend on his Nuptials 64

PROPERTIUS [SEXTUS PROPERTIUS] (d. after 16 BC):

    Cornelia from the Grave to Her Husband .. 188

RAINER MARIA RILKE (1875–1926):

    The Bride 44

    The Song of the Widow 195

EDWIN ARLINGTON ROBINSON (1869–1935):

    Eros Turannos . . , , ... 79

    Reuben Bright 191

DANTE GABRIEL ROSSETTI (1828–82):

    Nuptial Sleep 113

    For a Marriage of St. Catherine by Memling 213

WILLIAM SHAKESPEARE (1564–1616):

    Married Sounds 209

    'No Cause or Just Impediment' 217

    The Need of Posterity 221

    Wasted Beauty 223

PERCY BYSSHE SHELLEY (1792–1822):

    The Dreariest Journey 218

SIR PHILIP SIDNEY (1554–86):

    A Word Against Wives 222

CHRISTOPHER SMART (1722–71):

    Epithalamium on a Late Happy Marriage .. 63

EDMUND SPENSER (1552?–99):

To Her Doubts 25

Wedding Night 66

WALLACE STEVENS (1879–1955):

    The World as Meditation 168

    Life is Motion 205

JONATHAN SWIFT (1667–1745):

    The Progress of Marriage 98

ALFRED, LORD TENNYSON (1809–1892):

    Marriage Morning 39

    Tithonus 121

THEOCRITUS (b. *c.* 310 BC): The Suitor 19

DYLAN THOMAS (1914–53):

    On the Marriage of a Virgin 57

    On a Wedding Anniversary 134

MONA VAN DUYN (1921–):

    Toward a Definition of Marriage 234

EDMUND WALLER (1606–87):

    On the Two Dwarfs That Were Married at

        Court . . . . . . , ... 62

ROSANNA WARREN (1953–): Couple 77

WALT WHITMAN (1819–92): A Wedding Out West 56

RICHARD WILBUR (1921–): A Wedding Toast . . 65

WILLIAM CARLOS WILLIAMS (1883–1963):

    The Marriage of Souls 226

YVOR WINTERS (1900–68): The Marriage 135

GEORGE WITHER (1588–1667): A Widow's Hymn 194

JAMES WRIGHT (1927–80): Complaint 199